A New Twist on
TATTING
More Than 100 Glorious Designs

Love is like a Rose

A New Twist on TATTING

More Than 100 Glorious Designs

Catherine Austin

A Sterling\Chapelle Book

Sterling Publishing Co., Inc. New York

*Special thanks to Beth Reid for the loan
of many tatted pieces in this book, and to
Karla Rives and Nelda Fredrickson for the
loan of classic tatting created by their mother,
Mary Povey.*

Library of Congress Cataloging-in-Publication Data Available

10   9   8   7   6   5   4   3   2   1

Published by Sterling Publishing Company, Inc.
387 Park Avenue South, New York, N.Y. 10016
Produced by Chapelle, Ltd.
P.O. Box 9252, Newgate Station, Ogden, Utah 84409
© 1993 by Chapelle, Ltd.
Distributed in Canada by Sterling Publishing
c/o Canadian Manda Group, P.O. Box 920, Station U
Toronto, Ontario, Canada M8Z 5P9
Distributed in Great Britain and Europe by Cassell PLC
Villiers House, 41/47 Strand, London WC2N 5JE, England
Distributed in Australia by Capricorn Link Ltd.
P.O. Box 665, Lane Cove, NSW 2066
Printed in Hong Kong
All rights reserved

Sterling ISBN 0-8069-0289-2

For Chapelle, Ltd.

Owners
Jo Packham and
Terrece Beesley

Staff
Kathi Allred
Trice Boerens
Tina Annette Brady
Sandra Durbin Chapman
Holly Fuller
Kristi Glissmeyer
Jill Jensen
Susan Jorgensen
Margaret Shields Marti
Jackie McCowen
Barbara Milburn
Lisa Miles
Pamela Randall
Jennifer Roberts
Carol Sanders
Patricia Singleton
Florence Stacey
Lorrie Young
Nancy Whitley
Gloria Zirkel

Photographer: *Ryne Hazen*

Photographs in this book
were taken at
Anita Louise's Bear Lace
Cottage, Park City, Utah

Mary Gaskill's Trends &
Traditions, Ogden, Utah

Jo Packham's home,
Ogden, Utah

Edie Stockstill's home,
Salt Lake City, Utah

Their cooperation and trust
are deeply appreciated.

*This book is dedicated to the
lovliest and sweetest of daughters,
from a loving mother's heart.*

HISTORY OF TATTING

Tatting derives from the art of knotting, like macrame, which was popular throughout Europe in the 17th and 18th centuries. Rows of knots were worked with a shuttle and thread and the resultant cord was couched in various patterns onto fabric.

In the eighteenth century, when it was discovered how to form a fabric with this method, it evolved into what became known as tatting. Tatting was worked in silk, for preference, in various colors and was used in various decorative forms. It became widespread as a pastime in the nineteenth century when caps, collars, cuffs, doilies and edgings for all kinds of things were made of it.

The French call this work "frivolite"--frivolity. Eastern people call it "makouk", a name which means shuttle. And in Italy, it is called "chiacchierino", a word whose origin is uncertain but possibly derives from the word "chiacchierare", to gossip, the work being easily carried on while the daily gossip was being held.

In recent years, tatting was worked most often with a rather fine cotton in white or natural and was used in the place of crochet. It is a more solid and elegant lace than crochet but often times takes longer to create so it was frequently used in a combination with crocheted lace for decorative edgings for underwear and children's clothing. Today, among many needleworkers, there is a revival of the old art of knotted lace. These artisans are, however, using an entirely new kaleidoscope of fibers and have found many new and unusual end uses for traditional tatting patterns.

General Instructions

THE SHUTTLE

To work tatting, the small tool called a shuttle is necessary. The original shuttle was much larger than that in use today. An ordinary shuttle measures about three inches in length and one inch in width. It used to be made in wood or bone; today celluloid or plastic are the most common materials.

Inside the shuttle is a small reel with a hole through it. The thread is fixed through the hole and wound around the reel without, however, protruding beyond the edges of the shuttle (Diagram 1). This keeps the thread from getting dirty. When buying the shuttle, care should be taken that the two ends of the two halves of the shuttle fit perfectly. This assures that the thread is held tightly and firmly and cannot slip through, which is very inconvenient, especially when working with two shuttles.

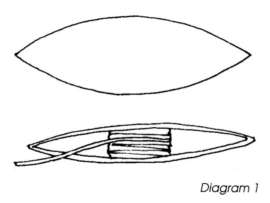

Diagram 1

When learning to tat, it is easier to wind the thread onto a shuttle and use this to pass the thread which forms the loops initially (that is, before transferring them) over the other thread which can be taken directly from the ball. These are known respectively as the shuttle thread and the ball thread.

To prepare the shuttle, place the end of the thread into the notch at the center of the shuttle and start winding the thread round until the shuttle is full but not projecting beyond the edge. Cut the thread, leaving a working length of about 16" (40 cm).

THE THREAD

Because it was traditionally intended to resemble other types of lace made by a more intricate method, tatting was usually worked in fine threads such as linen or cotton. For delicate work, these are still probably the most popular. Linen lace threads are less readily available and are more expensive than cotton which is made in a variety of weights, colors and textures. Wool and other knitting yarns are not as suitable for tatting, particularly for beginners, because they tend to stretch. However, a variety of contemporary fibers are available which give an entirely new twist to tatting and create a nice variation on a theme.

Heavier threads are not suitable for winding onto standard-size shuttles because they may damage the opening. Instead, simply wind the thread in a figure eight around your fingers and secure with a rubber band. It is then easy to let out more thread as needed.

The amount of thread required for any particular project is not usually easy to estimate because the length will vary with the tension of the individual worker. When working a pattern in individual motifs, however, it is possible to calculate how much thread will be required from the amount used for the first motif. To measure this, unravel several yards (meters) of thread and make a note of the exact measurement. Work the motif and measure the amount left. This, subtracted from the total amount, gives the length used in the motif.

METHOD OF WORKING TATTING

Tatting consists of a simple knot formed in two stages, making the basis of the lacework. Tatting can be done by hand or with a shuttle.

TATTING BY HAND

The stitch used throughout tatting, and the one from which all of the intricate patterns evolve, is in fact a simple knot. Its correct name is double reverse half hitch or lark's head but in tatting it is called a double stitch. This double stitch may be worked either to form a length, known as a chain, or to form rings. Most tatting patterns combine the two methods. Although the basic principle in working the chains and rings is the same, it is easier to start with a chain and progress to rings once the knack of forming the stitch is learned. It is advisable to start in string rather than cotton in order to see the formation of the stitch.

To make a practice length of about 3" (7.5cm), you will need: One 24" (60cm) length of string and one 6" (15cm) length. It is easier to start with two different colors.

To make the basic knot, double the shorter piece of string, loop it around the longer piece (Diagram 2) and pull the ends of the shorter piece through the loop. Tighten the resulting knot around the longer piece. Pick up the ends of the shorter piece and pull them straight out to the sides in opposite directions (Diagram 3). Pull tightly, allowing the ends of the longer piece to rise. As the length you are pulling straightens, the other length will form an identical knot around it which is known as the double stitch (Diagram 4).

This process shows the basic knot and how the loops are transferred. The next process shows how the knot is tied in two stages in tatting so that several stitches can be worked to form a chain.

To tie the knot in two stages, undo the first knot and re-tie it by wrapping the shorter length over the longer one, thus forming the knot in two motions (Diagram 5). Working over the hand, undo this second knot and tie the lengths together at one end with a simple overhand knot. Hold the knot between the fingers and thumb of your left hand and wrap the two lengths over the back of the fingers with the shorter length on the right. Work the first half of the double stitch with the shorter length (Diagram 6).

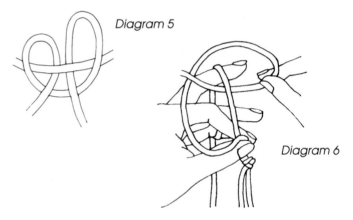

Diagram 5

Diagram 6

Pull the shorter length, or push the loop with your fingers, to transfer the loop so it is formed by the longer length (Diagram 7). Keeping the shorter length on the right, work the second half of the stitch with it (Diagram 8) and transfer the loop to the longer length (Diagram 9). Push the complete stitch along to the overhand knot. Work another stitch in the same way and push along each loop when transferred to the first stitch. Continue like this for the entire chain.

Diagram 3

Diagram 2

Diagram 4

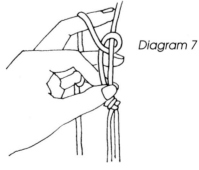

Diagram 7

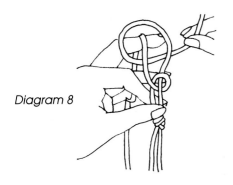

Diagram 8

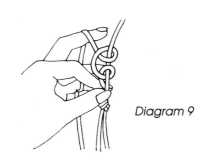

Diagram 9

When working a chain to form an edging, it is usually better to use thread of the same color because a different colored core shows between the stitches. However, you could use a thicker thread for the core which prevents confusion and gives a thicker edge for stitching the chain to fabric.

SPIRALS: A chain worked using one-half of the double stitch only will form an attractive spiral effect (Diagram 10). It does not matter which half of the stitch is worked as long as you are consistent.

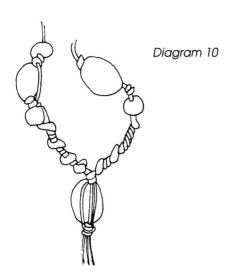

Diagram 10

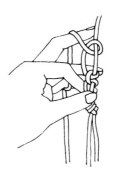

Diagram 11

PICOTS: These make an interesting addition to double stitches by forming loops between them. Make one double stitch in the normal way, then form the first half of a second stitch, pushing this one along to first stitch to leave a gap of 1/2" (12mm) between the two (Diagram 11). Complete the second half of the stitch and then push the entire stitch along to the first (Diagram 12). The gap between the two stitches forms a small loop. The size of the loop can be varied by leaving a smaller or larger gap between the stitches. Any number of stitches may be worked between picots.

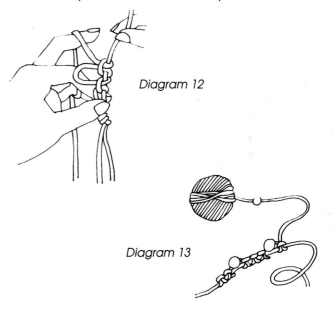

Diagram 12

Diagram 13

ADDING BEADS: Another unusual variation is to hang beads from the picots. To do this, thread the beads onto the longer piece of thread or ball thread and knot the end to prevent the beads from sliding off. Start making a picot in the normal way, sliding a bead along to the part of the thread which forms the gap between the double stitches. (Diagram 13).

TATTING WITH A SHUTTLE

After preparing the shuttle as described above, leave a length of thread free for 16"-20". Then, taking the end of the thread between finger and thumb of the left hand, wrap it around the other three fingers in a large circle (Diagram 14). Holding the shuttle in the right hand, pass it through the circle of thread from right to left (Diagram 15). Before moving the left hand, pull through the thread with the shuttle. Then, raising the third and fourth fingers of the left hand, slip the loop along the stretched thread (Diagram 16). Thus, the first movement has been worked, making half the complete knot. Diagram 17 shows a series of half knots left loose on the stretched thread. The beginner must learn this first movement very well and practice it often before attempting the second stage.

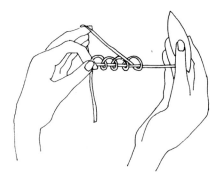

Diagram 17

The second half knot is worked in the opposite direction. After having wound the thread around the fingers of the left hand, as explained in the first stage, pass the shuttle, held in the right hand, from left to right through the circle (Diagram 18). With the right hand, as already explained in the first stage, hold the thread and remain still (Diagram 19) while the left hand closes up this second half knot, thus completing the whole knot (Diagram 20). On completion of the two stages, the whole process is begun again. Diagrams 21-23 show the looping of the thread to make the knots.

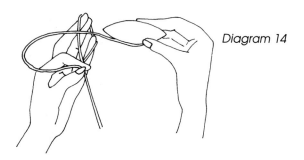

Diagram 14

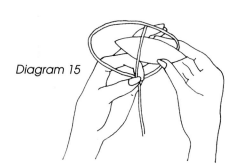

Diagram 15

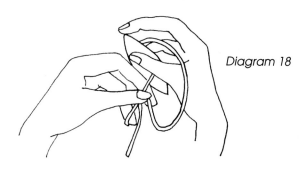

Diagram 18

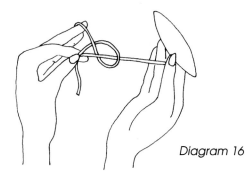

Diagram 16

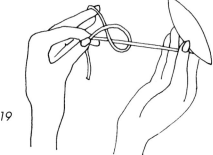

Diagram 19

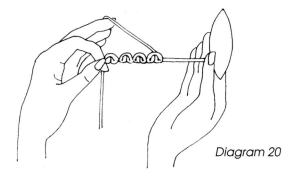

Diagram 20

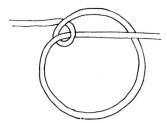

Diagram 21

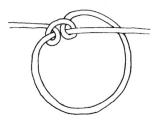

Diagram 22

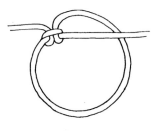

Diagram 23

The thread must always run freely through the knots which are formed. If the knots stick, it means that a stitch has been made incorrectly and the work must be begun again. Although tatting is easy, the work must be followed carefully and the knots counted with attention, keeping in mind that the work cannot easily be unpicked and that the whole effect of the work is spoiled if the thread has to be cut and knotted again.

After working the given number of knots necessary to form a circle, the basic circle is left free from the fingers of the left hand and the thread from the shuttle is slightly pulled in order to close up the circle.

TATTING WITH TWO SHUTTLES

Work with one shuttle produces a circle. If semi-circles or arcs are desired, two shuttles must be used. When working with two shuttles, proceed as follows: Knot the ends of the two threads and, to avoid confusing the shuttles, use two different colored threads. The thread from one shuttle passes over the middle and third fingers of the left hand, then it is wrapped twice around the little finger and left to fall free together with the shuttle (Diagram 24). Take the other shuttle in the right hand and work the same movements as if working with only one shuttle.

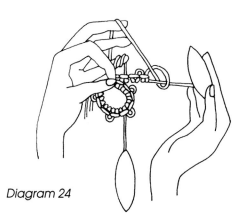

Diagram 24

13

ATTACHING CIRCLES AND ARCS TO PICOTS

In tatting, both circles and semi-circles are joined together at the point where there is a picot. To do this, pass the running thread from the left hand and through the picot, using a crochet hook or needle. Then push the shuttle through the loop which leaves the picot and draw up the thread before beginning the following knot (Diagram 25). Diagram 26 illustrates the attachment of picots.

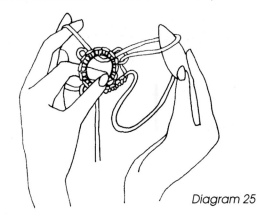

Diagram 25

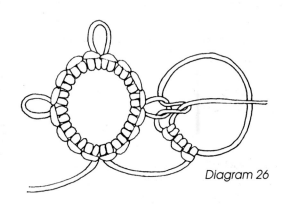

Diagram 26

JOINING THREADS

To join on thread in the course of the work, make a Weaver's Knot (see below), taking at least one of the threads through the next knot. The thread can never be joined when making a circle or arc, but only at the beginning or end.

SECOND METHOD OF WORKING TATTING

Diagrams 27 and 28 show another method of working tatting, a method which allows greater speed, especially for the expert. The shuttle first passes under and then over the loop of thread around the left hand while the thread is held tightly stretched by the little finger of the right hand. In this way, the length of thread from the shuttle to the work itself must be very much shorter than in the other method.

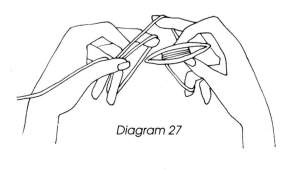

Diagram 27

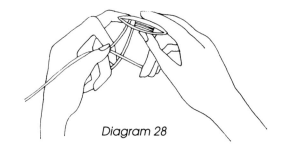

Diagram 28

NEEDLE TATTING

Thread needle with about 3 yards of thread. With left hand, place base of thread over ring, leaving 3" tail to tie at the end. With right hand, throw thread backward and insert needle front to back of ring (Diagram 29). Pull stitch into position and hold with left hand. Bring thread to the front of ring and insert needle back to front, bringing second half of stitch into position (Diagram 30). Repeat until ring is covered. Tie ends of thread together. Whip stitch or glue ends to back of ring (Diagram 31).

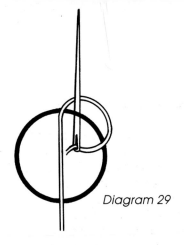

Diagram 29

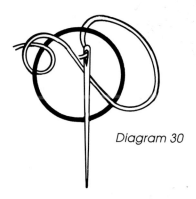

Diagram 30

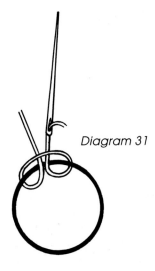

Diagram 31

Abbreviations

Double Stitch - ds: 2 half stitches made with the shuttle, forming one stitch.

Ring - r: The required number of double stitches made with the shuttle thread only and drawn into a ring.

Chain - ch: A scallop or cord made with the ball thread on the shuttle thread, not drawn up into a ring.

Picot - p: A loop left between stitches.

Close ring - cl r.

Definitions

Join: A loop drawn through a picot, shuttle passed through it, and thread drawn tightly, or with the ball thread or threads tied around.

Reverse work: Turn the work and continue as before, but in the opposite direction.

Sets of stitches: 4-4 or other numbers are single stitches of the stated number, like the first half of a ds, then the same number of single stitches, like the last half of a ds; this is one set of stitches.

GALLERY

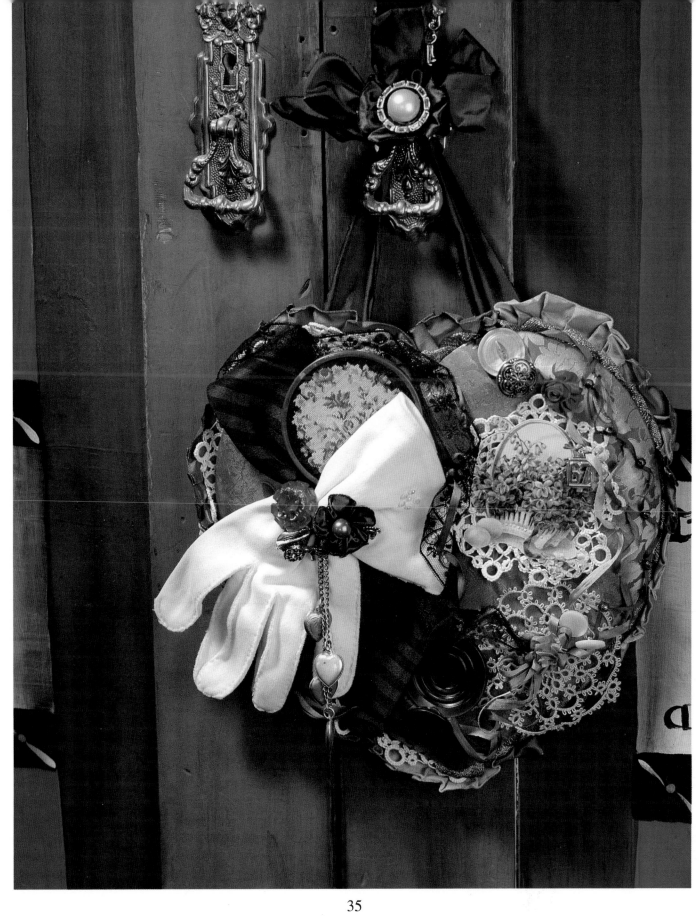

From the permanent collection of the
Museum of American Folk Art

PATTERNS

1

Tatted Tree

FINISHED SIZE
Approximately 2 1/2" wide x 4" high.

MATERIALS
DMC Cordonnet #50 (286-yd. ball): 1 Ecru.

TOOLS AND EQUIPMENT
One shuttle; one ball; size #10 steel crochet hook.

DIRECTIONS
Begin at base of tree: R of 3 ds, 3 p sep by 3 ds, 3 ds, cl r. Tie ball thread to shuttle thread.
* Ch of 3 ds, p, 3 ds. Reverse work.
R of 3 ds, join in last p of last r, 3 ds, 2 p sep by 3 ds, 3 ds, cl r. Reverse work.
Repeat from * 8 times = 10 r's sep by 9 ch's. Tie off.
Next row: R of 3 ds, p, 3 ds, join in p of first ch of previous row, 3 ds, p, 3 ds, cl r. Tie ball thread to shuttle thread.
* Ch of 3 ds, p, 3 ds. Reverse work.
R of 3 ds, join in last p of last r, 3 ds, join in p of next ch, 3 ds, p, 3 ds, cl r. Reverse work.
Repeat from * across row = 9 r's sep by 8 ch's. Tie off.
Continue in this same manner, working 1 ch and 1 r less in each row, until there are 2 r's and 1 ch at center top of tree.
Tree base: With shuttle only, r of 3 ds, 3 p sep by 3 ds, 3 ds, cl r.
R of 3 ds, join in last p of last r, 3 ds, p, 3 ds, join in p of 5th r in first row, 3 ds, cl r.
R of 3 ds, join in p of next (6th) r, 3 ds, 2 p sep by 3 ds, 3 ds, cl r.
R of 3 ds, join in last p of last r, 3 ds, 2 p sep by 3 ds, 3 ds, cl r. Tie last r thread to first r thread. Cut threads.

2

Blue Fringe

FINISHED SIZE
Approximately 2" wide.

MATERIALS
Marlitt (10m skein): 4 Dark Turquoise #1056.

TOOLS AND EQUIPMENT
2 shuttles.

DIRECTIONS
Note: Use 4 strands of thread throughout.
R of 4 ds, 3 p sep by 4 ds, 4 ds, cl r. Reverse work.
* Using both ball and shuttle threads, ch of 3 ds, (make a long p about 2 inches long, 1 ds) 8 times, 3 ds. Reverse work.
R of 4 ds, join to last p of last r, 4 ds, 2 p sep by 4 ds, 4 ds, cl r. Reverse work.
Repeat from * to desired length.
When completed, clip ends of p's even.
Handle: Make a ch of sets of sts: 4 single sts (the first half of ds), followed by 4 single sts (the 2nd half of ds). 4 - 4 is one set. Repeat sets to make ch 15" long or to desired length.

3

Needlecase Doll *(page 63)*

FINISHED SIZE
Approximately 3 5/8" wide x 5 1/2" high.

MATERIALS
DMC Pearl Cotton #8 (95-yd. ball): 1 Pink
Variegated #48.
1/8 yard of print fabric.
Scrap of white flannel.
Fusing material.
12" of 1/4"-wide ribbon.
6" of 1/2"-wide lace.
Manila folder.
Glue.

TOOLS AND EQUIPMENT
One shuttle.

DIRECTIONS
Bloomers (make 4): **Row 1:** R of 3 ds, 8 p sep by 1 ds, 3 ds, cl r.
* R of 3 ds, join to last p of previous r, 1 ds, 7 p sep by 1 ds, 3 ds, cl r.
Repeat from * 2 more times.
Row 2: R of 5 ds, 7 p sep by 1 ds, 5 ds, cl r.
* R of 5 ds, join to last p of previous r, 1 ds, 6 p sep by 1 ds, 5 ds, cl r.
Repeat from * 2 more times.
Dots (make 6): R of 8 ds, cl r. Tie off.
Flower bonnet - large ring: R of 3 ds, 7 p sep by 1 ds, 7 ds, cl r. Leave 1/8" tail.
* R of 3 ds, join to last p of previous r, 1 ds, 6 p sep by 1 ds, cl r.

Repeat from * 7 times.
R of 3 ds, join to last p of previous r, 1 ds, 5 p sep by 1 ds, join to first p of first r, 3 ds, cl r. Tie off.
Medium ring: R of 3 ds, 5 p sep by 1 ds, 3 ds, cl r.
* R of 3 ds, join to last p of previous r, 1 ds, 4 p sep by 1 ds, 3 ds, cl r. Leave 1/8" of thread.
Repeat from * 5 times.
R of 3 ds, join to last p of previous r, 1 ds, 3 p sep by 1 ds, 1 ds, join to first p of first r, 3 ds, cl r. Tie off.
Center flower: R of 1 ds, 8 p sep by 1 ds, 1 ds, cl r.
Repeat 4 times, making each r as close to the previous r as possible. Tie off.
Finishing: Make patterns for doll front, doll back and doll petticoat. Cut one front and one back from manila folder. On front piece only, cut horizontally at neck and trim away very small amount of folder. Following manufacturer's directions for use of fusing material, fuse print fabric to both sides of manila folder pieces, allowing the fabric for the front to become a hinge at the neck. Trim fabric to match edges of manila front and back. Glue petticoats to back. Glue heads of front and back together. Glue lace to bottom edge of skirt and across bonnet. Tie ribbon in bow around bonnet.
Glue two bloomer motifs on each leg of doll, one 1/4" above the other. Glue 5 dots spaced evenly on bottom of skirt. Glue last dot in center of bow. Glue large r for flower to front bottom of bonnet, then glue medium r, then center made with 4 r's to middle.

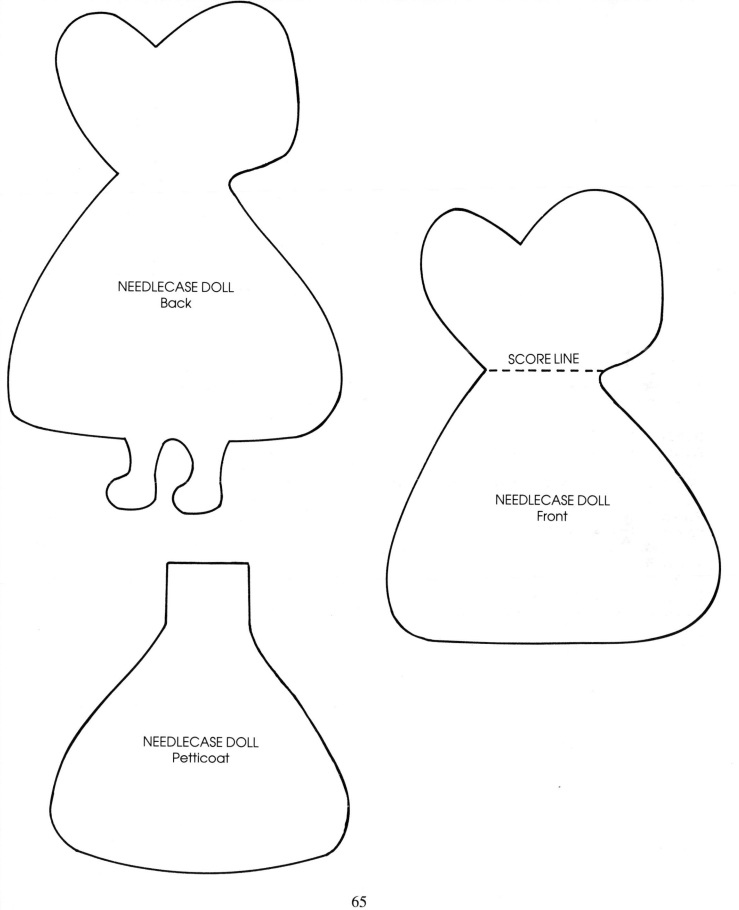

NEEDLECASE DOLL
Back

SCORE LINE

NEEDLECASE DOLL
Front

NEEDLECASE DOLL
Petticoat

65

4 *Blue Basket*

FINISHED SIZE
Approximately 3 1/4" high and 3" wide at the top.

MATERIALS
Fil D'Ecosse #16 (400m ball): 1 Pale Blue #152.

TOOLS AND EQUIPMENT
2 shuttles.

DIRECTIONS
Row 1: R of 3 ds, 5 p sep by 3 ds, 3 ds, cl r. Tie off to make a 6th p.
* Ch of 2 ds, p, 2 ds, join to first p. *
Repeat from * to *, make 6 ch.
Row 2: Ch of 3 ds, p, 3 ds.
Repeat around, joining in p of row 1.
Row 3: Ch of 4 ds, p, 4 ds.
Repeat around, joining in p of row 2.
Row 5: Ch of 5 ds, p, 5 ds (this forms the bottom of the basket). Join in p of row 3.
Stand of the basket: R of 4 ds, 3 p sep by 4 ds, 4 ds, cl r. Reverse work.
Ch of 5 ds. Reverse work.
R of 3 ds, join in last p of previous r, 4 ds, p, 3 ds, cl r. Reverse work.
Ch of 5 ds, join in last row. Reverse work.
Repeat large and small r's and ch's around, joining the p's on the outside of bottom, after making each 2nd ch.
Upper part: R of 4 ds, 3 p sep by 4 ds, 4 ds, cl r.

Reverse work.
Ch of 5 ds. Reverse work.
R of 3 ds, join last p of previous r, 2 ds, p, 2 ds, p, 3 ds, cl r. Reverse work.
Ch of 5 ds, join p of 3rd circle of bottom.
Repeat around.
Sides: R of 2 ds, 3 p sep by 2 ds, 2 ds, join 2nd p to p of last row, cl r. Reverse work.
Ch of 4 ds. Reverse work.
R of 4 ds, 5 p sep by 3 ds, 4 ds, cl r. Reverse work.
Ch of 4 ds. Reverse work.
R of 4 ds, 3 p sep by 4 ds, 4 ds, join first p to first r and 2nd p to bottom, cl r. Reverse work.
Ch of 4 ds. Reverse work.
R of 4 ds, join 2nd r, 4 p sep by 3 ds, 4 ds, cl r.
Repeat around.
Rim: R of 3 ds, 5 p sep by 3 ds, 3 ds, join 3rd p of a r in last row, cl r. Reverse work.
Ch of 3 ds, join last p of last r, 3 ds, 3 p sep by 2 ds, 3 ds, p, 3 ds, join 3rd p of next ring of last row.
R of 3 ds, 5 p sep by 3 ds, 3 ds, join first p to last p of ch.
Repeat around.
Handle: Ch of 6 ds, 13 p sep by 6 ds, 6 ds. Fasten to opposite side of basket. Ch back, joining each p with 6 ds between.
If the basket is made very firmly, it will not need stiffening. If desired, stiffen with a mixture of 3 parts water to one part glue.

5 Oval Doily

FINISHED SIZE
Approximately 11 1/2" wide x 15 1/2" long.

MATERIALS
DMC Cordonnet #40 (249-yd. ball): 1 Ecru.

TOOLS AND EQUIPMENT
2 shuttles.

DIRECTIONS
Tie threads at end of each row.

Row 1: * Small r of 2 ds, 3 p sep by 2 ds, 2 ds, cl r. Reverse work.
Ch of 5 ds. Reverse work.
Large r of 3 ds, 5 p sep by 2 ds, 3 ds, joining first p of new r to 3rd p of previous r. Reverse work.
Ch of 5 ds.
Repeat from * 12 more times, joining 2nd and following r's to first p of new r to 3rd p of previous r.
* * Large r of 3 ds, 5 p sep by 2 ds, 3 ds, cl r.
With other shuttle, make large r of 3 ds, join 5th p of previous r, 3 ds, 4 p sep by 2 ds, 3 ds, cl r.
Ch 5, join to 3rd p of last of 13 small r's made at the beginning.
Ch 5.
Using one shuttle, make 3 large r's as before, joining in the same manner as before.
Ch 5, join to same p on 13th small r where other ch was joined.
Ch 5.
Large r with one shuttle, 2nd large r made with other shuttle. Reverse work.
Ch 5, join to middle p of 13th small r. * *
Continue same as for first side, repeating from * * to * * on other end of original small r's.

Row 2: Begin on any ch in first row.
* Ch of 4 ds, 3 p sep by 2 ds, 4 ds. Reverse work.
R of 3 ds, join to middle p of large r's in first row, 3 ds, cl r. *
Repeat from * to * around, joining every large r in previous row.

Row 3: Repeat row 2.

Row 4: Repeat row 2.

Row 5: * R of 2 ds, join any middle p of any ch on row 4, 2 ds, cl r. Reverse work.
Ch 5.
R of 2 ds, 5 p sep by 2 ds, 2 ds, cl r.
Ch 5. Reverse work. *
Repeat from * to * around.

Row 6: * Ch of 4 ds, 5 p sep by 1 ds, 4 ds.
R of 2 ds, 2 p sep by 2 ds, 2 ds, join middle p of r on previous r, 2 ds, 2 p sep by 2 ds, 2 ds, cl r. *
Repeat from * to * around.

Row 7: Using one shuttle, * r of 4 ds, 2 p sep by 2 ds, 2 ds, cl r.
R of 3 ds, join to 2nd p of previous r, 2 ds, 5 p sep by 1 ds, 2 ds, p, 3 ds, cl r. Join first p to 2nd p of previous r.
R of 2 ds, join to last p of previous r, 2 ds, p, 4 ds, cl r.
Ch of 4 ds, 2 p sep by 1 ds, 1 ds, join to any ch on row 6, 1 ds, 2 p sep by 1 ds, 4 ds. *
Repeat from * to * around, joining every ch in row 6.

Row 8: R of 4 ds, join to any middle p of large r on previous row.
Long ch of 15 ds, p, ch 9. Reverse work.
* R of 3 ds, p, 3 ds, 5 p sep by 1 ds, 3 ds, p, 3 ds, cl r.
Using 2nd shuttle, make same r, joining first p to last p of previous r. Reverse work. *
Ch of 15 ds.

Clover leaf: Using one shuttle, r of 3 ds, 3 p sep by 3 ds, 3 ds, cl r.
R of 3 ds, join to last p of previous r, 3 ds, 5 p sep by 1 ds, 3 ds, p, 3 ds, cl r.
R of 3 ds, join to last p of previous r, 3 ds, 2 p sep by 3 ds, 3 ds, cl r. Reverse work.
Ch of 15 ds.
Repeat from * to *, joining 6th p of new r's with 6th p of corresponding r's made earlier.
Ch of 9 ds, join to p in first long ch, ch of 15 ds.
Repeat from beginning of row 8, joining every other r on previous row.

FINISHED SIZE
Leaf: 1 5/8" x 3"
Bud: 3/4" diameter

MATERIALS
Schewe Fil D'ecosse # 16 (400m ball): 1 each
Salmon #142, Light Olive #140.
Fine-covered florist's wire.
Mill Hill Glass seed beads #00275.
Antique glass beads #03029.

TOOLS AND EQUIPMENT
Tatting shuttle; size 9 steel crochet hook; fingernail polish.

DIRECTIONS
Rose centers: With crochet hook and size 20 corchet cotton, chain 3, join to first stitch making a ring. 8 double crochets in ring, join to 1st dc. * 1 dc in each dc around, repeat from * for 3 rows, joining at the first of each row. Stuff. dc 2 together all around. Finish off leaving 8-10" of thread for a tail. Cut a piece of wire about 10" long and slip end through end of ball. Wrap other end of wire around end of ball also. Poke wire end of ball inside with stuffing, then sew ball around wire hiding the end.

Rose petals: With size 50 crochet cotton make a ring of 30 picots separated by 1 1/2 ds's close tightly. On end of pink thread paint end with fingernail polish and let dry. (This makes a needle to thread beads on.) Thread 96 beads on. Join to picot of ring, * Chain of 2 ds, p, 1ds, p, 3 beads with one p between each bead. P, then 1ds, p, 1ds, p, 2ds. Join to next picot on ring, making 1st petal. Skip next 3 picots on ring and join in next picot, repeat from * until there are six petals.

Row 2: After sixth petal of 1st row, sl st thread to p atleft of first petal, then work as in 1st row, * making chain of 2 ds, 3p, 5 beads with 1 p between, 3 p, 2 ds, join to 1st p on right side of first petal*. This forms first petal of 2nd row. Skip one picot and sl st in picot on left of next petal of 1st row. Repeat between * and join as before. Continue around r to complete 2nd row. There should now be 1 p between petals all around r.

Row 3: * sl st to 1st p, chain 2 ds, 4 p, 8 beads with 1 p between each, 4 p, 2 ds, join to next p between petals, repeat from * around to complete row. This brings the three rows of petals in direct line with each other from the center. Slide the base ring onto the crocheted ball about 1/2 way and sew in place.

Buds: First make crocheted ball as for rose, finishing it with wire stem, and winding end of thread around base for bulb of flower. * Chain 4 ds, bead, p, alternating bead, and p, until there are 7 beads then 3 picots graduated in size the first and last being 1/8", the center one 1/4", 7 beads with 1 p, between each, 4ds. Bring ends of chain together, pass shuttle thread over and ball thread under start of chain and make another ds to hold in place making a petal. Make a ring of 2 ds, 4 p's, 3 graduated picots as before, 4 p's, 2 ds. Close. Repeat from * until there are 4 chains and 4 rings, then join to 1st chain around ball. Sew chains in place on top of ball and let the rings hang down freely.

Finishing: Drop roses in hot water and let dry. (This shrinks the thread and helps it to hold its shape.) Then starch roses with any stiffiner and adjust petals while drying.

Leaf Cluster: Cut two pieces wire each 6" and one 8" long. Cover these wires with green crochet cotton in double crochet, leaving 1/2" of wire at each end.

Tatted edge of leaf: Join threads at beginning of crochet covering, work 3 ds, 3 p's, (graduated in size as before) separated by 1 ds, 3 ds, join to fourth st from first joining, repeat all around. Bring the ends of each wire together at beginning of covering and wind to cover ends of threads.

Tatted center of leaves: Paint end of green thread with fingernail polish and let dry. String 54 beads for each small leaf and 62 beads for large leaf. For small leaves make 1 small ring, 2 large rings, 1 small ring. For large leaf add 5th ring on end after last small ring. Sew chain of rings to inside of leaves by hooking picots to bottom of dc's.

Small ring: Before making ring of thread around left hand slide up 8 beads on ring around left hand, 2 ds, 4 beads with 1 p between, 2 ds, p, 2ds, 4 beads with 1 p, between, 2 ds. Close. Slide 3 beads up next to ring and then join shuttle thread to center picot.

(Continued on page 142)

7

Border & Edging Set

FINISHED SIZE

Pillowcase insertion approximately 1 3/8" wide and pillowcase edging approximately 3/4" wide. Sheet insertion approximately 1 3/4" and sheet edging approximately 1 1/2".

MATERIALS

Pillowcase: DMC Cordonnet #70 (361-yd. ball): 1 White. Sheet: DMC Cordonnet #50 (286-yd. ball): 1 White.

TOOLS AND EQUIPMENT

2 shuttles.

DIRECTIONS

Pillowcase edging: Row 1: R of 4 ds, 3 p sep by 4 ds, 4 ds, cl r. Reverse work.

* Ch of 7 ds, p, 7 ds. Reverse work.

R of 4 ds, join to last p of previous r, 4 ds, 2 p sep by 4 ds, 4 ds, cl r. Reverse work.

Repeat from * to desired length.

Row 2: R of 4 ds, 3 p sep by 4 ds, 4 ds, cl r. Reverse work.

* Ch of 7 ds, join to middle p of r on row 1, 7 ds. Reverse work.

R of 4 ds, join to last p of previous r, 4 ds, 2 p sep by 4 ds, 4 ds, cl r. Reverse work.

Ch of 7 ds, join to middle p of next r on previous row, 7 ds. Reverse work.

R of 4 ds, join to last p of last r, 4 ds, 2 p sep by 4 ds, 4 ds, cl r. Reverse work.

Ch of 7 ds, join to next p of previous r, 11 ds, p, 7 ds. Switch shuttles. Do not reverse work.

R of 4 ds, 3 p sep by 4 ds, 4 ds, cl r.

Ch of 7 ds. Reverse work.

First clover leaf: R of 4 ds, p, 4 ds, join to middle p of 3rd r made, 4 ds, p, 4 ds, cl r.

R of 4 ds, join to last p made, 6 ds, 2 p sep by 6 ds, 4 ds, cl r.

R of 4 ds, join to last p, 4 ds, 2 p sep by 4 ds, 4 ds, cl r. Reverse work.

Ch of 7 ds, join to last p of 2nd shuttle r, 7 ds. Reverse work.

2nd clover leaf: R of 9 ds, join to middle p of last r on previous clover leaf, 4 ds, p, 4 ds, cl r.

R of 4 ds, join to last p of previous r, 7 ds, 2 p sep by 7 ds, 4 ds, cl r.

R of 4 ds, join to last p of previous r, 4 ds, p, 9 ds, cl r.

Reverse work.

Ch of 7 ds, join to middle p of 2nd shuttle r, 7 ds. Reverse work.

3rd clover leaf: R of 4 ds, p, 5 ds, join to last p of last r on 2nd clover leaf, 5 ds, p, 4 ds, cl r.

R of 4 ds, join to last p of previous r, 6 ds, 2 p sep by 6 ds, 4 ds, cl r.

R of 4 ds, join to last p of previous r, 4 ds, 2 p sep by 4 ds, 4 ds, cl r. Reverse work.

Ch of 7 ds, join to first p of 2nd shuttle r, 7 ds, join to p on opposite ch, 11 ds, skip next p of previous row and join to next p, 7 ds. Reverse work.

R of 4 ds, p, 4 ds, join to middle p of last r on 3rd clover leaf, 4 ds, p, 4 ds, cl r. Reverse work.

Repeat from * of row 2 to end.

Pillowcase insertion: Row 1: R of 3 ds, 3 p sep by 6 ds, 3 ds, cl r. Reverse work.

Ch of 8 ds. Switch shuttle.

With 2nd shuttle, r of 6 ds, 3 p sep by 6 ds, 6 ds, cl r. Switch shuttle. Do not reverse work.

Ch of 8 ds. Reverse work.

Clover leaf: R of 2 ds, p, 3 ds, join to last p of first r, 2 ds, p, 3 ds, cl r.

Large r of 4 ds, join to last p of small r, 5 ds, 2 p sep by 5 ds, 4 ds, cl r.

Repeat first r, joining first p to last p of large r. Reverse work.

Ch of 8 ds. Switch shuttle.

With 2nd shuttle, r of 6 ds, join to last p of adjacent r, 6 ds, 2 p sep by 6 ds, 6 ds, cl r. Switch shuttle.

Ch of 8 ds. Reverse work.

Repeat from beginning of row 1 to desired length.

Row 2: Repeat row 1, joining middle p of 2nd shuttle r's of both rows.

Rows 3 and 4: Ch of 6 ds, p, 6 ds, join to middle p of next large r.

Ch of 6 ds, p, 6 ds, join to middle p of middle r of clover leaf.

Repeat from beginning of row 3 to desired length. Repeat row 4 on opposite side.

Sheet Insertion: Using one shuttle, * r of 4 ds, 3 p sep by 4 ds, 4 ds, cl r. Leave 1/4" of thread.

Small r of 4 ds, p, 4 ds, cl r. Leave 1/4" of thread.

R of 4 ds, join 3rd p of previous r, 4 ds, 2 p sep by 4 ds, 4 ds, cl r. Leave 1/4" of thread.

73

Small r of 4 ds, join to p on previous small r, 4 ds, cl r. Leave 1/4" of thread. *

Repeat from * to * to desired length.

Make 2nd side in the same manner as the first, joining small r's to p on first side where small r's are joined.

Join to fabric by middle p's of larger r.

Sheet edging: * R of 4 ds, 3 p sep by 4 ds, 4 ds, cl r. Leave 1/4" of thread.

Small r of 3 ds, p, 3 ds, cl r. Leave 1/4" of thread.

R of 4 ds, join 3rd p of previous r, 4 ds, 2 p sep by 4 ds, 4 ds, cl r. Leave 1/4" of thread.

Large r of 3 ds, join to p of small r, 3 ds, 3 p sep by 1 ds, 3 ds, p, 3 ds, cl r. Leave 1/4" of thread.

R of 4 ds, join 3rd p of previous r, 4 ds, 2 p sep by 4 ds, 4 ds, cl r. Leave 1/4" of thread.

Small r of 3 ds, join to last p of large r, 3 ds, cl r. Leave 1/4" of thread. *

Repeat from * to * to desired length.

8

Salmon Edging & Flowers

FINISHED SIZE
Approximately 1/2" wide.

MATERIALS
DMC Pearl Cotton #3 (16.25-yd. skein): 1 Peach #353. DMC tatting thread (106-yd. ball): 1 Apricot #754. Balger by Kreinik 1/16" ribbon (5m spool): 2 Gold/Apricot #021.
Braided cording: 2/3 yard.

TOOLS AND EQUIPMENT
2 shuttles.

DIRECTIONS
Lace around edge: With tatting thread, * r of 2 ds, 7 p sep by 1 ds, 2 ds, cl r. Reverse work.
Ch of 4 ds, 3 p sep by 12 ds, 4 ds, join to middle p of previous r, 4 ds. Reverse work.
R of 2 ds, 7 p sep by 1 ds, 2 ds, cl r. Reverse work.
Ch of 4 ds. *
Repeat from * to * to desired length, joining first p of new ch to 3rd p of previous ch.

Flower petals: With pearl cotton, * r of 1 ds, 16 p sep by 1 ds, cl r. *
Repeat from * to * 4 more times, joining first p of new r to last p of previous r. Tie off.
R of 1 ds, 5 long p sep by 1 ds, 1 ds, cl r. Tie off, leaving 1" off thread.
With metallic ribbon, * r of 1 ds, 25 p sep by 1 ds, 1 ds, cl r. *
Repeat from * to * 4 more times, joining first p of new r to last p of previous r. Tie off.
* R of 1 ds, 5 p sep by 1 ds, 1 ds, cl r. *
Repeat from * to * 2 more times, do not join first p to last r. Tie off. Leave 1" of thread.
Arrange flower bouquet having metallic large flower circle with large peach flower circle on top. Small peach flower and metallic flowers are drawn through center of other 2 circles by tails of thread. Gather several metallic loops and sew them and flowers to fabric.

9

Fisherman's Net Doily

FINISHED SIZE
Approximately 13" diameter.

MATERIALS
Coats and Clark Three Cord #30 (350-yd. ball): 1 White.

TOOLS AND EQUIPMENT
One shuttle.

DIRECTIONS
Center: R of 2 ds, 10 p sep by 2 ds, 2 ds, cl r. Tie off.

Row 1: * R of 5 ds, join to any p on center r, 5 ds, cl r. Leave 1" of thread.

Large r of 5 ds, p, 5 ds, p, 1 ds, p, 5 ds, p, 5 ds, cl r. Leave 3/8" of thread.

Large r of 5 ds, join last p on previous large r, 5 ds, p, 1 ds, p, 5 ds, p, 5 ds, cl r. Leave 1" of thread. * Join. Tie off.

Repeat from * to * 9 more times.

Row 2: * R of 5 ds, join to 2nd p on any large r of row 1, 5 ds, cl r. Leave 1" of thread.

Large r of 5 ds, p, 5 ds, p, 1 ds, p, 5 ds, p, 5 ds, cl r. Leave 1" of thread.

R of 5 ds, join to first p of next large r in row 1, 5 ds, cl r. Leave 1" of thread.

Large r of 5 ds, join last p of previous large r, 5 ds, p, 5 ds, p, 5 ds, cl r. Leave 1" of thread. *

Repeat from * to * around, being sure to join last r with first r made on row. Join. Tie off.

Row 3: R of 5 ds, join any r on row 2 with one free p, 5 ds, cl r. * Leave 1" of thread.

Large r of 5 ds, p, 5 ds, p, 1 ds, p, 5 ds, p, 5 ds, cl r. Leave 1" of thread.

R of 5 ds, join first free p of next r of row 2, 5 ds, cl r. Leave 1" of thread.

R of 5 ds, join last p of previous large r, 5 ds, 2 p sep by 5 ds, 5 ds, cl r. Leave 1" of thread.

R of 5 ds, join 2nd p of same ring as before, 5 ds, cl r. *

Repeat around from * to *, alternating r's with 3 and 4 p's around, joining each free p of row 2. Join. Tie off.

Row 4: * R of 5 ds, join any p of row 3, 5 ds, cl r. Leave 1" of thread.

Large r of 5 ds, 3 p sep by 5 ds, 5 ds, cl r. Leave 1" of thread. *

Repeat from * to *, joining all free p's of row 3 and p's of large r's. Join. Tie off.

Row 5: Ch of 5 ds, 3 p sep by 1 ds, 5 ds, join to p of large r of row 4.

Repeat ch around edge of doily. Join. Tie off.

10 *Mauve Embellishment*

FINISHED SIZE
Approximately 9" wide, 7" long at center.

MATERIALS
Rowan Designer Collection Cabled Mercerised Cotton (160m ball): 1 ball Pale Mauve #311.

TOOLS AND EQUIPMENT
One shuttle; one ball.

DIRECTIONS
Use ball and shuttle. Do not cut thread between.
R of 3 ds, 3 p sep by 2 ds, 3 ds. Reverse work.
Ch of 5 ds, p, 3 ds. Reverse work.
R of 5 ds, join last p of r, 5 ds, cl r. Reverse work.
Ch of 3 ds, 2 p sep by 3 ds, 3 ds. Reverse work.
R of 5 ds, join middle p of first r, 5 ds, cl r. Reverse work.
Ch of 3 ds, p, 5 ds, join last p of first r.
* Ch of 5 ds, p, 5 ds, join base of first r.
Ch of 5 ds, p, 5 ds, join p in first ch.
Ch of 2 ds, 3 p sep by 2 ds, 2 ds, join p of next ch.
Ch of 2 ds, 5 p sep by 2 ds, 2 ds, join next p of same ch.
Ch of 2 ds, 3 p sep by 2 ds, 2 ds, join next p.
Ch of 5 ds, p, 5 ds, join between next 2 ch. Leave 1/16" of thread.
Repeat from beginning 3 times.
When making next 3 quarters of large medallion, join ch's at corresponding p's. A 3/4 square makes the point below large square, joined to large square at p on 2 outer most ch's of large square. Make first quarter of point as above, the other 2 as follows: eliminate ch marked with asterisk and instead ch of 4 ds, join to base of first r, continue square same as above.

Oval motif: Do not cut thread between ball and shuttle. Make 2 motifs with each motif having 10 rings.
Center r of 2 ds, 10 p sep by 2 ds, 2 ds, cl r.
R of 3 ds, 3 p sep by 8 ds, 3 ds, cl r. Join to p of center.
R of 3 ds, join last p of first r, 6 ds, p, 6 ds, p, 3 ds, cl r. Join center r, repeat last ring 3 times, then one like the first ring (one with 8 ds) and 4 more like the 2nd r (6 ds), joining p's each time and joining last r with first r at the last p. Tie off.

Edging: Start at first 6 ds ring of oval, join to p at top of that r, ch of 3 ds, p, 3 ds, join to first ch below corner on large square.
Ch of 3 ds, p, 3 ds, join next p on oval.
Repeat ch, joining at p between small squares and next ch. Continue with 3 ds, 3 p sep by 3 ds, 3 ds around oval, join at beginning p, ch of 3 ds, 3 p sep by 3 ds, 3 ds, join at middle p of ch forming corner.
Continue across top, joining same as for first side.
Continue ch's around 2nd oval same as for first oval. Tie off.
Join threads at joint where oval and square are hooked together by ch and continue with ch of 3 ds, 3 sep by 3 ds, 3 ds around point, joining at middle p of ch's around point.

11

Beaded Edging

FINISHED SIZE
Approximately 1 1/4" wide.

MATERIALS
Avocet Soiree'(94m ball): 1 each White, Peach #505, Aqua #520.

Pearlized beads (6mm): Light Green, Light Peach, White.

TOOLS AND EQUIPMENT
2 shuttles.

DIRECTIONS
R of 4 ds, 3 p sep by 4 ds, 4 ds, cl r. Reverse work.
* Ch of 7 ds, p, 7 ds. Reverse work.
R of 6 ds, join to 3rd p of previous r, 6 ds, cl r.
R of 6 ds, p, 6 ds, cl r. Repeat 2 times, turn.
Ch of 7 ds, p, 7 ds. Reverse work.
R of 4 ds, join to p of last r, 4 ds, 2 p sep by 4 ds, 4 ds, cl r.
Repeat from * around. Tie off.
Sew beads to 7 ds ch's at the p.

12

Scalloped Doily (page 82)

FINISHED SIZE
Approximately 8 1/2" diameter.

MATERIALS
DMC Cordonnet #50 (286-yd. ball): 1 Ecru.

TOOLS AND EQUIPMENT
2 shuttles.

DIRECTIONS
Flower: R of 3 ds, 8 p sep by 3 ds, 3 ds, cl r.
R of 2 ds, 3 p sep by 12 ds, 2 ds, cl r. Join to any r on center.
* R of 2 ds, join to last p of previous r, 12 ds, 2 p sep by 12 ds, 2 ds, cl r. *
Repeat from * to * around center, joining next p on center after each r and joining first r with last r. Join. Tie off.
Row 1: Using one shuttle, * r of 4 ds, p, 4 ds, join to a p of previous row, 4 ds, p, 4 ds, cl r. Reverse work. Leave 1/8" thread.
R of 4 ds, 3 p sep by 4 ds, 4 ds, cl r. Reverse work. Leave 1/8" thread. Reverse work.
R of 4 ds, join last p of first r made, 4 ds, 2 p sep by 4 ds, 4 ds. Reverse work. Leave 1/8" thread.
R of 4 ds, join to last p of 2nd r made, 4 ds, 2 p sep by 4 ds, 4 ds. Leave 1/8" thread. Reverse work.
R of 4 ds, join 3rd p of 3rd r made, 4 ds, 2 p sep by 4 ds, 4 ds, cl r. Reverse work. Leave 1/8" thread.
R of 4 ds, join to 3rd p of 4th r made, 4 ds, 2 p sep by 4 ds, 4 ds. Leave 1/8" thread. Reverse work. *
Repeat from * to * 7 more times, joining last r's with first r's. Tie off.
Row 2: Make 8 flowers, joining 2 petals to free p's on row 1, leaving a free p between the petals.
Join 2nd and remaining flowers to next petal of previous flower and join last flower with first. Join threads at beginning of row. Tie off.
Row 3: Repeat row 1, joining middle p's of r's to 2 petals opposite those joined to row 1. Leave 6 r's not joined at middle p between flowers.
Row 4 (scallop on outer edge): * * Ch of 6 ds, join to any free p on previous row, 6 ds.
* R of 3 ds, p, 3 ds, join to next free p on previous row, 3 ds, 5 p sep by 3 ds, 3 ds, cl r. Reverse work. Ch of 2 ds, 5 p sep by 2 ds, 2 ds. *
Repeat from * to * 5 more times, eliminating 6th ch, joining 6th p of last r to 4th free p on previous row (from last joining to previous row - this leaves 3 free p's between). * *
Repeat from * * to * * 11 more times = 12 scallops. Join threads at beginning of row. Tie off.

13
Blue Edging

FINISHED SIZE
Approximately 7/8" wide.

MATERIALS
DMC embroidery floss (8.7-yd. skein): 2 Medium Blue #799.

TOOLS AND EQUIPMENT
2 shuttles.

DIRECTIONS
Note: Use 6 strands of floss throughout.
* R of 4 ds, 2 p sep by 4 ds, 8 ds, cl r. Reverse work.
Ch of 8 ds, p, 8 ds, join to 2nd p of r. *
Repeat from * to * to desired length.

14
Tatted Pansy

FINISHED SIZE
Approximately 2 1/4" diameter.

MATERIALS
DMC Flower thread (21.8-yd. skein): 1 each Dark Mauve #2315, Light Mauve #2316, Light Yellow #2745, Ecru.

TOOLS AND EQUIPMENT
2 shuttles.

DIRECTIONS
Wind a very little light yellow on the shuttle, and make a r of 3 ds, 5 p sep by 3 ds, 3 ds. Tie off.
Small petal: Wind shuttle with dark mauve, without cutting thread, join to a p, ch of 2 ds, 13 p sep by 2 ds, 2 ds, join into same p, ch of 2 ds, 11 p sep by 2 ds, 2 ds, join into center p of first ch.
Ch of 2 ds, 11 p sep by 2 ds, 2 ds, join into same p in the r.
Middle petal: Join thread into next p of r.
Ch of 2 ds, 15 p sep by 2 ds, 2 ds, join into p in r.
Ch of 2 ds, 13 p sep by 2 ds, 2 ds, join into center p of previous ch.
Ch of 2 ds, 13 p sep by 2 ds, 2 ds, join into p in r.
Large petal: Carry threads to next p in r, ch of 2 ds, 17 p sep by 2 ds, 2 ds, join in same p.

Ch of 2 ds, 15 p sep by 2 ds, 2 ds, join in center p of previous ch.
Ch of 2 ds, 15 p sep by 2 ds, 2 ds, join in same p in center r.
Carry threads to next p in r.
Repeat large petal, then middle petal. Tie off.
Wind shuttle with light mauve, join into p at starting point.
Small petal: Ch of 2 ds, 3 p sep by 2 ds, 2 ds, join in 3rd p of the ch.
Make 8 small scallops around the petal. Carry thread to next petal, make 10 scallops; on the large petal make 12 scallops. The 2 large petals have 2 rows of scallops, the 2nd has 13 scallops, but with 2 p's in first and last scallops.
Wind shuttle with ecru and work around each petal; first and last scallops of 6 ds, the others 11 ds.
Do not press the work, but arrange with your fingers. Overlap the petals as shown in the diagram. In fastening on the goods to decorate, tack lightly so as not to flatten the work, as the effect is much more natural if left loose. Different markings may be used as desired. Make the stems with silk as near the natural color as possible.
Ch of ds to desired length and tie to the pansy on the wrong side.

FINISHED SIZE
Approximately 5" x 7".

MATERIALS
DMC Pearl Cotton #5 (48m ball): 1 Slate Green #926. Watercolors by Caron (40-yd. skein): 2 Abalone #051.
Glass beads (500 count package): 1 package #00252.
2 pieces florist's fine covered wire.

TOOLS AND EQUIPMENT
One shuttle; size 11 crochet hook.

DIRECTIONS
Body: Row 1: Ch 2, 5 dc in first ch, join to first dc.
Row 2: 2 Dc in ea st around.
Row 3: Dc, sk 1 st, dc in ea st around.
Row 4: 2 Dc in ea st around.
Rows 5 and 6: Dc in ea st. Stuff after row 6.
Row 7: Dc, sk 1 st, dc, join to first of row. Fasten off.
Antenna: Tat a 2" long ch of double sts. Pull slightly, so there is a little curve.
Wings: Use fine covered fine wire for the foundation. For the larger wings, cut the wire into a 18" piece, for the small wings, cut the wire into a 12" piece. Make a sharp bend at center of longer wire, which will go a little below the head on the crocheted body. Fasten temporarily while shaping on either side of the body, bring ends of wire together, lap 1/3" under body about 1/2" lower than center of wire. Make slight bend in center of short wire, bring ends around to center in long loops, lap as before. Fasten to center bend to form smaller wings. After fastening ends of both wires, bend them into proper shape for the outline of each pair of wings, then remove from body and leave ends free while covering wire. Cover wire of both pairs of wings very closely with sc.
Tatted edge: Join threads about 1/2" from end of wire to crochet cover, 2 ds, 3 p sep by 1 ds, 2 ds, center p longer than others, join to 4th st on wire from first joining. Continue around both pairs of wings.
Bottom wings: Make a ch of half sts 4-4 sets, 4 first half knots, picot, 4 2nd half knots until there are 11 p's on each side (every other p should flip upside down).
R of 2 ds, 11 p sep by 1 ds, 2 ds, cl r.
Sew to the smaller wire covered with tatted edge, sewing p's to the side.
Large wings: 6 Ch of r's, each as follows: r of 2 ds, 17 p sep by 1 ds, 2 ds, cl r.
Carry thread through center of r and join to center p of r just made.
R of 2 ds, 15 p sep by 1 ds, 2 ds, cl r. Join thread to center p as before.
R of 2 ds, 13 p sep by 1 ds, 2 ds, cl r, end in same manner as before.
R of 2 ds, 11 p sep by 1 ds, 2 ds, cl r, end in same manner.
Sew r ch's in place through the p's, sewing the 3 smaller r's at the end of each ch to center of the wings overlapping slightly.
Sew bottom set of wings to larger wings.
Sew body on top of wings.
Sew antenna to back of head.
Sew beads for eyes and around neck, placing them randomly around body, as desired.

16 *Cuff*

FINISHED SIZE
Approximately 3 1/4" wide.

MATERIALS
DMC Cordonnet #50 (286-yd. ball): 1 White.

TOOLS AND EQUIPMENT
2 shuttles.

DIRECTIONS
Make strips separated by the fill-in motif for desired length.

Strip: R of 7 ds, p, 7 ds, cl r. Join with ball thread.
Ch of 4 ds, 3 p sep by 4 ds, 4 ds. Reverse work.
R of 7 ds, join p of last r, 7 ds, cl r. Reverse work.
Ch of 4 ds, 3 p sep by 4 ds, 4 ds. Reverse work.
R of 7 ds, join to same p where last r is joined, 7 ds, cl r.
* R of 7 ds, p, 7 ds, cl r. Reverse work.
Ch of 4 ds, 3 p sep by 4 ds, 4 ds. Reverse work.
R of 7 ds, join to p of last r, 7 ds, cl r. *
Repeat from * to * 4 times.
Ch of 4 ds, 3 p sep by 4 ds, 4 ds. Reverse work.
R of 7 ds, join to p where last 2 previous r's are joined, 7 ds, cl r. Reverse work.
Ch of 4 ds, 3 p sep by 4 ds, 4 ds. Reverse work.
R of 7 ds, join to p where 3 other r's are joined, 7 ds, cl r. Reverse work.
* * R of 7 ds, join to where next 2 r's on first side are joined, 7 ds, cl r. Reverse work.
Ch of 4 ds, 3 p sep by 4 ds, 4 ds. Reverse work.
R of 7 ds, join to where 3 p's are joined, 7 ds, cl r. Reverse work. * *
Repeat from * * to * * 3 times.
R of 7 ds, join to last group of 3 p, 7 ds, cl r. Reverse work.
Ch of 4 ds, 3 p sep by 4 ds, 4 ds, join to base of very first r. Tie off.

Fill in motif: R of 7 ds, p, 7 ds, cl r. Reverse work.
Ch of 4 ds, p, 4 ds, join to middle p of last ch made on last strip, 4 ds, p, 4 ds. Reverse work.
R of 7 ds, join to p of last r, 7 ds, cl r. Reverse work.
* Ch of 4 ds, p, 4 ds, join middle p of next ch on strip, 4 ds, p, 4 ds. Reverse work.
R of 7 ds, p, 7 ds, cl r. Reverse work.
Ch of 4 ds, p, 4 ds, join middle p of next ch on strip, 4

ds, p, 4 ds. Reverse work.
R of 7 ds, join to p of last r, 7 ds, cl r. Reverse work. *
Repeat from * to * once more.
Ch of 4 ds, p, 4 ds, join to middle p of last ch on strip, 4 ds, p, 4 ds. Reverse work.
R of 7 ds, p, 7 ds, cl r. Reverse work.
Ch of 4 ds, 3 p sep by 4 ds, 4 ds. Reverse work.
R of 7 ds, join to p of last r made, 7 ds, cl r. Reverse work.
Ch of 4 ds, p, 4 ds, join to middle p of first ch on 2nd strip, 4 ds, p, 4 ds. Reverse work.
* * R of 7 ds, join to p where next 2 p's on other side are joined, 7 ds, cl r. Reverse work.
Ch of 4 ds, p, 4 ds, join to middle p of next ch of 2nd strip, 4 ds, p, 4 ds. Reverse work.
R of 7 ds, join to p where 3 r's are joined, 7 ds, cl r. Reverse work.
Ch of 4 ds, p, 4 ds, join to middle p of next ch, 4 ds, p, 4 ds. Reverse work. * *
Repeat from * * to * * once.
R of 7 ds, p, 7 ds, cl r. Reverse work.
Ch of 4 ds, p, 4 ds, join to last p on ch of 2nd strip, 4 ds, p, 4 ds. Reverse work.
R of 7 ds, join to p of last r, 7 ds, cl r. Reverse work.
Ch of 4 ds, 3 p sep by 4 ds, 4 ds. Reverse work.
R of 7 ds, join to where last 2 r's are joined, 7 ds, cl r. Reverse work.
Ch of 4 ds, 3 p sep by 4 ds, 4 ds. Reverse work.
R of 7 ds, join to where last 3 r's are joined, 7 ds, cl r. Reverse work.
Ch of 4 ds, 3 p sep by 4 ds, 4 ds. Reverse work.
R of 7 ds, join to p of 2nd group of 4 r's, 7 ds, cl r. Reverse work.
Ch of 4 ds, 3 p sep by 4 ds, 4 ds. Reverse work.
R of 7 ds, join to p, joining the first 2 r's made, 7 ds, cl r. Reverse work.
Ch of 4 ds, p, 4 ds.
R of 7 ds, join p of ch of corresponding ch on previous motif, 7 ds, cl r.
Ch of 4 ds, p, 4 ds. Reverse work.
R of 7 ds, join to last group of 3 r's, 7 ds, cl r. Reverse work.
Ch of 4 ds, 3 p sep by 4 ds, 4 ds, join to base of first r made. Tie off.

17

Purse Clasp

FINISHED SIZE
Approximately 3" wide x 6" long.

MATERIALS
DMC Cebelia #30 (515m ball): 1 White.
2 (3/4") plastic rings, 2 (5/8") plastic rings, 1 (1/2") plastic ring.

TOOLS AND EQUIPMENT
2 shuttles.

DIRECTIONS
Before tatting, needle tat around rings, using same thread as used for tatting.
Around one of the medium-sized rings (makes the wheel): * R of 3 ds, p, 3 ds, join to covered center r, 3 ds, p, 3 ds, cl r. Reverse work.
Ch of 4 ds, 5 p sep by 4 ds, 4 ds. Reverse work. *
Repeat from * to * 9 more times, until there are 10 r's and 10 ch's, joining 2 of the ch's to the 2nd covered medium plastic ring by the middle p's.

Fasten the smaller plastic ring above the 2nd medium ring with needle and thread.
Around the wheel and 2 plastic rings are r's and ch's as in the wheel, but ch's are of 4 ds, 3 p sep by 4 ds, 4 ds.
R is made in the same manner. Join the middle p of r's to middle p of ch's on previous row.
Join 6 r's to small plastic r, 2 r's on each side of first medium r and 14 around wheel.
For upper part: sew the 2 largest r's together. Join 3 clover leaves to each r, beginning where r's are joined and spacing them around the large r. Join to r by first and last p's of first and 3rd r's of clover leaf.
Clover leaf: R of 5 ds, 5 p sep by 3 ds, 5 ds, cl r.
R of 5 ds, join to last p of previous r, 5 ds, 4 p sep by 3 ds, 5 ds, cl r.
R of 5 ds, join to last p of previous r, 5 ds, 4 p sep by 3 ds, 5 ds, cl r.
Join last r of 3rd clover leaf (both sides) to top 2 r's around smallest plastic ring.

18

Varigated Daisy Spray (page 92)

FINISHED SIZE
Flowers approximately 1 5/8" wide.

MATERIALS
Watercolors by Caron (40-yd. skein): 1 Slate.
Mill Hill glass seed beads: 1 package #00374.

TOOLS AND EQUIPMENT
2 shuttles.

DIRECTIONS
Use one thread throughout. The daisies are made separately.
With a continuous thread, ch a short stem of a p and 10 or 12 sets of 4-4 sts.
Ch of 16 ds, 3 long p sep by 2 ds, 16 ds.
Form into a loop, crossing at its beginning, shuttle thread over, ball thread under the ch, work 2 ds, draw shuttle thread very tight (this forms the first petal).
Make 7 petals very close together. Join in a r with the first petal and sew neatly to the stem.
Stem and leaves: Ch 12 sets of 5-5 sts, p, 5 sets of 4-4 sts, reverse, 2 ds, 13 p sep by 2 ds, draw tightly, join p and form a leaf.
Join a daisy by the p left on the stem. Make a set of 4-4 sts and carry shuttle thread around the daisy to hold it firmly.
Join daisies and leaves on opposite sides of the stem. Make the stem the desired length of 5-5 sts. Make another leaf and daisy. Leaving the p in the center of a set of sts will bring it on the opposite side. Finish the spray with a daisy at the end of the stem.

19

Candle Shade (page 93)

FINISHED SIZE
Approximately 4 1/2" wide.

MATERIALS
DMC Cordonnet #50 (286-yd. ball): 1 White.
Mill Hill Antique Glass Beads (250 count package): 2
packages #03017.

TOOLS AND EQUIPMENT
2 shuttles.

DIRECTIONS
Triangle: Clover leaf: R of 4 ds, 5 p sep by 4 ds, 4 ds,
cl r.
R of 4 ds, join last p of previous r, 4 ds, 4 p sep by 4
ds, 4 ds, cl r.
R of 4 ds, join last p of previous r, 4 ds, 4 p sep by 4
ds, 4 ds, cl r. Reverse work.
Ch of 7 ds, p, 7 ds. Reverse work.
Repeat clover leaf, joining 2nd p of new r to 4th p of
last r of previous clover leaf and continue in same
manner as first clover leaf.
Ch of 7 ds, join to p of previous ch, 7 ds. Reverse
work.
Repeat clover leaf, joining first r as before and
joining 4th p of 3rd r to 4th p of first r made in first
clover leaf.
Wheel: Center: R of 2 ds, 10 long p, 2 ds, cl r. To
make the long p's even, make them over a 7/8"
wide cardboard strip. Make a circle of 10 r's. Tie off.
* R of 8 ds, p, 8 ds, cl r. Reverse work.
Ch of 2 ds, 2 p sep by 2 ds, 2 ds, join to p of center r,
2 ds, 2 p sep by 2 ds, 2 ds, join p of r just made.
Ch of 4 ds. Reverse work.
Repeat from * 9 more times, joining p's of center r.
After 10th joining of ch to p, reverse work, ch of 5 ds,
join to base of r just made.
Ch of 2 ds, 4 p sep by 2 ds, 2 ds, join to 4th p of first r
of left clover leaf (hold triangle of clover leaves so
there is one at the top and 2 on the bottom, join first
joining to left clover leaf), 2 ds, 2 p sep by 2 ds, 2 ds,
join to p of same r on wheel.
+ Ch of 5 ds, join to next r.
Ch of 2 ds, 2 p sep by 2 ds, 2 ds, join to 2nd p of 3rd r
of next clover leaf, 2 ds, 4 p sep by 2 ds, 2 ds, join p

of same r. +
Ch of 5 ds, join to next r.
Repeat ch's from + to + and r's around wheel,
except make ch's of 2 ds, 7 p sep by 2 ds, 2 ds. Tie
off.
Edging around wheel and triangle: * R of 6 ds, p, 6
ds, cl r. Reverse work.
Ch of 2 ds, 3 p sep by 2 ds, 2 ds, join to p of r. *
Repeat from * around 5 more times.
Hold center motif so the triangle of clover leaves is
at the top.
R of 6 ds, p, 6 ds, cl r. Reverse work.
Ch of 2 ds, p, 2 ds, join to 3rd p of first r in top clover
leaf (on left side of clover leaf), 2 ds, p, 2 ds, join to p
at end of r.
Repeat r and ch, joining ch to 2nd p of next large r
in the adjoining clover leaf.
Repeat r and ch, joining ch to middle p of next r in
same clover leaf.
Repeat from * to * once.
* * Repeat r and ch, joining ch to middle p of first
free r and ch of wheel. * *
Repeat from * to *.
Repeat from * * to * * to next ch on wheel.
Repeat from * to * 3 more times.
(R of 6 ds, join to middle p of next free ch on wheel,
6 ds, cl r.
Ch of 2 ds, 3 p sep by 2 ds, 2 ds, join to same p as
previous r, 2 ds, 3 p sep by 2 ds, 2 ds, join to base of
r). Reverse work.
Repeat from * to * 3 times.
Repeat between ( ) once.
Repeat from * to * 3 times.
Repeat between ( ) once.
Repeat from * to * 3 times.
Repeat between ( ) once.
Repeat from * to * 3 times.
Repeat r and ch, joining ch to middle p of next ch
on wheel.
Repeat from * to * once.
Repeat r and ch, joining ch to middle of next ch on
wheel - should be the last free ch on wheel.
Repeat from * to * once.
Repeat next 3 r's and joining ch as were the first 3 on
opposite side of clover leaf.

Tie threads together with beginning threads and cut. This makes one complete panel.

Join next panel to first, following same pattern of r and ch.

On the side by the first panel, join by ch's from first clover leaf to 3rd ch on wheel, then continue in the same manner as the first panel with r's and ch's.

Outside row: Count the number of 6 ds, p, and r's along bottom and top and multiply by 4 to determine how many beads to string. Fill the shuttle with beads, pushing the beads back on the thread. Ch of 2 ds, slide one bead close to the ds, 4 times in all, 2 ds with one bead following, join base of r. Use the beads only at the top and bottom, omitting them on the r's which join the panels. Make 5 of the panels.

Finishing: Tea dye candle shade to desired color. Rinse in vinegar water, then rinse in clear water. Stiffen with a mixture of 3 parts water to one part glue. Block and allow to dry.

20 *Yellow-Petaled Flower* (page 96)

FINISHED SIZE
Approximately 4 3/4" diameter.

MATERIALS
DMC Pearl Cotton #8 (87m ball): 1 Light Yellow #745.
Milliners fine covered wire: 36" piece.

TOOLS AND EQUIPMENT
2 shuttles.

DIRECTIONS
Cut a 6" piece of wire for each of the 6 petals. Cover each piece of wire closely with dc, beginning and ending 1/2" from ends.

Edge: Join threads at beginning of crocheted covering, 2 ds, 5 p sep by 2 ds, 2 ds, join 5th st in crochet from first joining. Continue across whole length of wire, bring ends together and fasten.

Center of petals: With shuttle thread, make clover leaf: r of 4 ds, p, 3 ds, 3 p sep by 1 ds, 3 ds, p, 4 ds, cl r. Make lock stitch by drawing loop of shuttle thread under connecting thread, pass shuttle through loop, draw close. Leave a little thread between this r and next r.

R of 4 ds, p, 3 ds, 5 p sep by 1 ds, 3 ds, p, 4 ds, cl r. Lock stitch, join at first p of the first r.

Repeat first r. Leave 1/4" thread.

Make r on opposite side from last r made: r of 5 ds, join first p, first r of clover leaf, 4 ds, 3 p sep by 1 ds, 4 ds, p, 5 ds, cl r. Leave 1/4" thread.

Repeat on the other side and join.

Continue from one side to the other until there are 5 pairs of r's besides the clover leaf, each a little smaller than the preceding pair, so the petals grow narrower toward the base. Fasten in position in wired outer edge with pins, then sew p's to under side of wire with fine thread. Spread the wire loops so that the inside work will fit tight, that the fagoting between r's may be effective.

Center: Large r of 2 ds, 10 p sep by 2 ds, cl r. Surround by small scallops, ch of 3 ds, 5 p sep by 2 ds, 3 ds.

Arrange petal around center, wind closely to cover all wire, bend petals to suit taste.

21 Black Flower (page 99)

FINISHED SIZE
Approximately 5 1/2" wide and 8" high.

MATERIALS
DMC Cebelia #10 (258m ball): 1 Black #310.

TOOLS AND EQUIPMENT
2 shuttles.

DIRECTIONS
Top of flower: Leave a p at the beginning, ch of 3 ds, 12 p sep by 3 ds, 3 ds, 9 ds (this forms the scroll before the first upper petal). Reverse work.
Ch of 2 ds, join p of scroll, 2 ds, 8 p sep by 2 ds, 2 ds, join last p of scroll. Reverse work.
Ch of 5 ds, for space between petals, p, 10 ds, join 5th p of first petal.
Ch of 2 ds, 10 sep by 2 ds, 2 ds, join p of ch.
Make 3 more petals, increasing by one the number of ds and p's. The last ch at the end of the petals is of 3 ds only.

For the other half, begin with the scroll, at 9th p, join 9th p of first scroll, continue in same manner as before.
Outside row of tatting cords: Join thread in first p of first petal, make a ch of 4 sets of 4-4 sts, join first p of next petal, continue until the 5th petal, then make 10 sets and join last ch of 3 ds.
Center of flower: Make a loop: ch of 5 ds, 26 p sep by 2 ds, 5 ds, join by crossing ch, draw closely, make a stem with ch of sets of 4-4 sts. Sew all ends of threads that are left very closely.
Leaf cluster on stem: P, 3 ds, p, 10 ds. Reverse work. Ch of 2 ds, 10 p sep by 2 ds, join p.
Loop: ch of 5 ds, 15 p sep by 2 ds, 4 ds, join by crossing ch, draw closely, 1 ds, p, 1 ds.
Make leaf in the same manner as the other, joining after 10 ds to last p made, then 3 ds, join p of beginning, 3 ds, then ch of sets of 4-4 sts and join to long stem.
Repeat for the other leaf cluster, making it a little larger with 12 p on leaves, 21 p on loop.

22 American Flag

FINISHED SIZE
Approximately 15 1/2" x 11 1/4"

MATERIALS
DMC Pearl cotton #8 (53-yd ball): 3 each Red #666, White.
DMC Pearl cotton (27-yd. skein): 4 Dark Blue #820.
2 1/4" yds. of 3/4" cream lace.
Fifty 3/8" white buttons.
24" stick.

TOOLS AND EQUIPMENT
4 shuttles; size #12 steel crochet hook.

DIRECTIONS
Blue background: Using blue, * R 3 ds, 3 p sep by 3 ds, 3 ds, cl r RW Repeat r.
** Leave 1/4" thread. R 3 ds, join to last p of 1st r made, 3 ds, 2 p sep by 3 ds, 3 ds, cl r RW. R 3 ds, join to last p of 2nd r made, 3 ds, 2 p sep by 3 ds, 3 ds, cl r, RW. After making each set of double r's (after the 1st set), do the following: Slip crochet hook under the prev 1/4" thread (from the bottom of thead), catch the thread from the shuttle and pull a loop of thread to the front of the r's. Slide the shuttle through the loop and pull thread tightly. Then continue from ** until there are 20 double r's. Tie off. This makes one strip. Make 5 more strips, joining the 2nd p of 1st r, 3rd r, etc to 2nd p of r on prev strip, tie each strip off.
Red stripes: With red, *Repeat r's as done in blue, except join 1st p of 1st r to 3rd p of r at end of blue strip. Join 2nd r to next blue r and continue strip until there are 27 double r's. Tie off. Skip one blue strip and repeat from *. Make a total of 4 red strips.
Make 3 separate long red strips of 47 double r's.
White stripes: Hand stitch lace to red strips and blue area by p's.
Stars: R 3 ds, 5 p sep by 3 ds, 3 ds, cl r tie off. Make 50 stars. Glue to blue area (alternate rows of 6 stars and 5 stars) and glue 1 button on top of each star. Insert straight stick on left side of flag, weaving under and over the 1/4" threads.

98

23

Tatted Frog

FINISHED SIZE
Approximately 5 1/2" wide x 3" high.

MATERIALS
DMC Pearl Cotton #8 (95-yd. ball): 2 Rose #223.

TOOLS AND EQUIPMENT
2 shuttles.

DIRECTIONS
When working scroll section, you need 2 shuttles to work in a continuous coil. A shuttle will hold about 9 yards of thread, so when winding shuttles, wind the first off the ball of thread, then unwind 9 yards and wind it on the 2nd shuttle. Do not cut thread in between shuttles.

Frog: Round coil of p, 12 ds, join p.

Row 2: Coil of 24 ds, join to first p.

Rows 3-6: Sets of 4-4 sts all around, join to start of coil. Be sure to pull shuttle thread tightly to give crimped effect.

Button loop: Add a 3rd thread to make this. Ball thread and 3rd thread pass around the hand alike, keep the thread separated on the fingers and do not cross them in using. With the 3rd thread, make 1 ds, reverse by dropping that thread from 3 fingers, retaining it between the thumb and finger, with the ball thread, make one ds, reverse and make one ds with the 3rd thread to desired length.

Scroll section: One p, * 30 ds. Reverse shuttles, 15 p sep by 3 ds, 3 ds, join p at beginning. Repeat from * for opposite scroll.

Join in the center, make another pair of scrolls of 35 ds, 3 ds, 17 p sep by 3 ds, 3 ds. Repeat for opposite scroll. Draw the shuttle thread tightly around the center of both pairs and close firmly.

For the center scroll, make a ch of one p, 16 sets of 4-4 sts, loop it by crossing the threads over the ds ch at the beginning.

Ch of 6 ds, 24 p sep by 2 ds, 6 ds, loop this ch by crossing at the beginning.

For the cord through the center, 8 sets 4-4 sts. Sew to center. **Buttons:** Cover button molds with 2 thicknesses of white silk.

Row 1: One p, 12 ds, join p.

Row 2: Make a row of 4-4 sts and sew to position.

Row 3: A row of sets of 4-4 sts with p after each set.

Row 4: Join first p, 3 ds, p, 3 ds, join next p, continue, there should be 10 small scallops.

Row 5: Join p, make 2 sets 4-4 sts, p.

2 sets more, join next scallop, repeat around. Fasten ends neatly, and sew motif to covered mold under the end.

Oval coils (make 2): One p, 10 sets of 4-4 sts, p, 12 sets of 4-4 sts, loop the 12 sets crossing the ch after the last p, shuttle thread over, ball thread under the ch.

Make 10 sets of 4-4 sts, join p at beginning. Make 2 more rows around the oval, joining the p's at top and beginning. Sew to under side of work.

Assembly: Pass the first pair of scroll leaves through the oval coils, the 2nd pair over the ovals and sew to them.

24 *Red Heart*

FINISHED SIZE
Approximately 3 1/2" wide x 3 1/4" high.

MATERIALS
DMC Pearl Cotton #8 (95-yd. ball): 1 Rose Variegated #107.

TOOLS AND EQUIPMENT
One shuttle; one ball.

DIRECTIONS
R of 6 ds, large p, 6 ds, cl r. Tie ball thread to shuttle thread.
Ch of 4 ds, 5 p sep by 2 ds, 4 ds. Reverse work.
* R of 6 ds, join to large p, 6 ds, cl r. Reverse work.
Ch of 4 ds, 5 p sep by 2 ds, 4 ds. Reverse work.
Repeat from * 4 times. Join at base of first r. Tie off.
R of 6 ds, large p, 6 ds, cl r. Tie ball thread to shuttle thread.
Ch of 4 ds, 2 p sep by 2 ds, 2 ds, join to center p of a ch on first motif, 2 ds, 2 p sep by 2 ds, 4 ds. Reverse work.
Repeat from *.
R of 6 ds, large p, 6 ds, cl r. Tie ball thread to shuttle thread.
Ch of 4 ds, 2 p sep by 2 ds, 2 ds, join to center p of next ch on first motif, 2 ds, 2 p sep by 2 ds, 4 ds. Reverse work.
R of 6 ds, join to large p, 6 ds, cl r. Reverse work.
Ch of 4 ds, 2 p sep by 2 ds, join to center p of next ch on 2nd motif, 2 ds, 2 p sep by 2 ds, 4 ds. Reverse work.
Repeat from *.
Join ball and shuttle threads to the last p of joined ch on 3rd motif, join to first p of next ch.
Ch of 3 ds, 3 p sep by 2 ds, 3 ds, join to middle p of same ch, ch of 3 ds, 3 p sep by 2 ds, 3 ds. Reverse work.

R of 3 ds, p, 3 ds, join to first p of next ch, 3 ds, p, 3 ds, cl r. Reverse work.
Ch of 3 ds, 3 p sep by 2 ds, 3 ds. Reverse work.
R of 3 ds, join to last p of last r, 3 ds, join to middle p of same ch, 3 ds, p, 3 ds, cl r. Reverse work.
Ch of 3 ds, 3 p sep by 2 ds, 3 ds. Reverse work.
R of 3 ds, join to last p of last r, 3 ds, join to last p of same ch, 3 ds, p, 3 ds, cl r. Reverse work.
Ch of 3 ds, 3 p sep by 2 ds, 3 ds. Reverse work.
R of 3 ds, join to last p of last r, 3 ds, join to 2nd p of next ch, 3 ds, p, 3 ds, cl r. Reverse work.
Ch of 3 ds, 3 p sep by 2 ds, 3 ds. Reverse work.
R of 3 ds, join to last p of last r, 3 ds, skip one p of ch, join to next p of same ch, 3 ds, p, 3 ds, cl r. Reverse work.
Ch of 3 ds, 3 p sep by 2 ds, 3 ds. Reverse work.
R of 3 ds, join to last p of last r, 3 ds, join to 2nd p of next ch, 3 ds, p, 3 ds, cl r. Reverse work.
(Ch of 3 ds, 3 p sep by 2 ds, 3 ds. Reverse work.
R of 3 ds, join to last p of last r, 3 ds, 2 p sep by 3 ds, 3 ds, cl r. Reverse work.) twice.
Ch of 3 ds, 3 p sep by 2 ds, 3 ds. Reverse work.
R of 3 ds, join to last p of last r, 3 ds, join to middle p of next ch, 3 ds, p, 3 ds, cl r. Reverse work.
Ch of 3 ds, 3 p sep by 2 ds, 3 ds. Reverse work.
R of 3 ds, join to last p of last r, 3 ds, skip 1 p, join in next p of same ch, 3 ds, p, 3 ds, cl r. Reverse work.
Ch of 3 ds, 3 p sep by 2 ds, 3 ds. Reverse work.
Make 2 more r's in this same manner, joining to 2nd and 4th p of next ch, separate the r's with a ch as before.
Make another ch in this same manner.
You are now at the half way point. Work up the other side of heart in the same manner as for the first side, joining in same p's as on the first side.
End by joining last p of last ch and first p of joining ch together. Tie off.

25

Medallion Edging

FINISHED SIZE
Approximately 3 1/4" wide.

MATERIALS
DMC Cebelia #30 (515m ball): 1 Ecru.

TOOLS AND EQUIPMENT
One shuttle.

DIRECTIONS
Row 1: R of 4 ds, 5 p sep by 2 ds, 4 ds, cl r. Reverse work. Leave 1/8" of thread.
R of 4 ds, 5 p sep by 2 ds, 4 ds, cl r. Reverse work. Leave 1/8" of thread.
* R of 4 ds, join to last p on first r, 2 ds, 4 p sep by 2 ds, 4 ds, cl r. Reverse work. Leave 1/8" of thread.
R of 4 ds, join to last p on 2nd r, 2 ds, 4 p sep by 2 ds, 4 ds, cl r. Reverse work. Leave 1/8" of thread. *
Repeat from * to * to desired length. Tie off.
Row 2 (small motif): R of 4 ds, p, 4 ds, join to middle p of first r on previous row, 4 ds, p, 4 ds, cl r.
R of 4 ds, join to last p of previous r, 4 ds, 2 p sep by 4 ds, 4 ds, cl r.
R of 4 ds, join to last p of previous r, 4 ds, 2 p sep by 4 ds, 4 ds, cl r.
R of 4 ds, join to last p of previous r, 4 ds, p, 4 ds, join to first p of first r, 4 ds, cl r.
Repeat this motif as many times as needed to join

every other r on previous r. Be sure to join 2nd p of 2nd r to 2nd p of 4th r of previous motif. Tie off each one.
Row 3 (first large motif): **Center:** R of 1 ds, 15 p sep by 1 ds, 1 ds, cl r. Tie off.
* R of 5 ds, join to any p of center r, 5 ds, cl r. Reverse work. Leave 1/8" of thread.
R of 4 ds, 5 p sep by 2 ds, 4 ds, cl r. Reverse work. Leave 1/8" of thread. *
R of 5 ds, join to next p of center r, 5 ds, cl r. Reverse work. Leave 1/8" of thread.
R of 4 ds, join to last p of previous r, 2 ds, p, 2 ds, join to free p of 2nd small motif made, 2 ds, 2 p sep by 2 ds, 4 ds, cl r. Reverse work. Leave 1/8" of thread.
R of 5 ds, join next p of center r, 5 ds, cl r. Reverse work. Leave 1/8" of thread.
R of 4 ds, join last p of previous r, 2 ds, p, 2 ds, join to free p of first small motif made, 2 ds, 2 p sep by 2 ds, 4 ds, cl r. Reverse work. Leave 1/8" of thread.
Repeat from * to * around center r, having 15 small and 15 large r's, joining first p of each r to previous r and last p of 15th r to first p of first r. Tie off.
2nd and following large motifs: Work same as for first motif, but leave one r between joinings to 2nd row. Skip one r from 2nd joining to 2nd row and join 2 corresponding r's on first large motif.
The last large motif is joined to row 2 in the same manner as the first large motif.

26 *Ecru Doily*

FINISHED SIZE
Approximately 9 3/4" diameter.

MATERIALS
DMC Cebelia #30 (563-yd. ball) 1 Ecru #619.

TOOLS AND EQUIPMENT
2 shuttles.

DIRECTIONS
Tie off at the end of each row.

Row 1: R of 2 ds, 5 p sep by 2 ds, 2 ds, cl r. Reverse work.

Ch of 3 ds, 3 p sep by 2 ds, 3 ds. Reverse work.

* R of 2 ds, p, 2 ds, join 4th p of previous r, 3 p sep by 2 ds, 2 ds, cl r. Reverse work.

Ch of 3 ds, 3 p sep by 2 ds, 3 ds. *

Repeat from * until there are 8 r's and 8 ch's.

Row 2: * R of 3 ds, p, 3 ds, join to first p of any ch of first row, 3 ds, p, 3 ds, cl r. Reverse work.

Ch of 5 ds, p, 5 ds. Reverse work.

R of 3 ds, p, 3 ds, join to 3rd p of same ch, 3 ds, p, 3 ds, cl. Reverse work.

Ch of 5 ds, p, 5 ds. *

Repeat from * around, being sure to join r's at first and 3rd p of ch's of first row.

Row 3: * R of 3 ds, p, 3 ds, join to p of any ch on row 2, 3 ds, p, 3 ds, cl r. Reverse work.

Ch of 3 ds, 3 p sep by 2 ds, 3 ds. *

Repeat from * around.

Row 4: * Small r of 3 ds, p, 3 ds, join first p of any ch of row 3, 3 ds, p, 3 ds, cl r. Leave 1/8" of thread.

Large r of 4 ds, 3 p sep by 4 ds, 4 ds, cl r. Leave 1/8" of thread.

Small r of 3 ds, join to 3rd p of previous r, 3 ds, join to middle p of same ch of row 3, 3 ds, p, 3 ds, cl r. Leave 1/8" of thread.

Large r of 4 ds, join last p of previous large r, 4 ds, 2 p sep by 4 ds, 4 ds, cl r. Leave 1/8" of thread.

Small r of 3 ds, join to 3rd p of previous r, 3 ds, join to last p of same ch, 3 ds, p, 3 ds, cl r. Leave 1/8" of thread.

Large r of 4 ds, join last p of previous large r, 4 ds, 2 p sep by 4 ds, 4 ds, cl r. Leave 1/8" of thread.

Repeat from * to * around.

Row 5: * Ch of 4 ds, 3 p sep by 2 ds, 4 ds. Reverse work.

R of 3 ds, p, 3 ds, join p of large r of row 4, 3 ds, p, 3 ds, cl r. Reverse work. *

Repeat from * to *, joining every other large r of 4th row.

Row 6: Repeat row 4.

Row 7: Repeat row 5.

Row 8: * R of 3 ds, p, 3 ds, join to first p of any ch of row 7, 3 ds, p, 3 ds, cl r. Leave 1/4" of thread.

Small r of 3 ds, p, 3 ds, cl r. Leave 1/4" of thread.

R of 3 ds, join last p of previous r, 3 ds, join 2nd p of same ch, 3 ds, p, 3 ds, cl r. Leave 1/4" of thread.

Large r of 4 ds, join p of small r, 7 ds, 2 p sep by 7 ds, 4 ds, cl r. Leave 1/4" of thread.

R of 3 ds, join last p of previous r, 3 ds, join to 3rd p of same ch, 3 ds, p, 3 ds, cl r. Leave 1/4" of thread.

Small r of 3 ds, join to last p of large r, 3 ds, cl r. Leave 1/4" of thread. *

Repeat from * to * around.

27 Daisy Border

FINISHED SIZE
Approximately 1 1/8" wide.

MATERIALS
DMC Flower thread (21.8-yd skein): 1 each Green #2469, Yellow #2726.

TOOLS AND EQUIPMENT
2 shuttles.

DIRECTIONS
Leaflet: R of 9 ds, p, 5 ds, p, 14 ds, cl r.
R of 14 ds, p, 5 ds, p, 9 ds, cl r. Reverse work.
Ch of 16 ds. Reverse work.
Daisy: Ring 1: R of 10 ds, join first p of first r, 4 ds, p, 4 ds, p, 10 ds, cl r.
Ring 2: R of 10 ds, join last r, 8 ds, p, 10 ds, cl r. Join all r's.
Repeat r 2, 2 times.
Repeat r 1, 2 times.
Repeat r 2, omitting the last p. Reverse work.
Ch 15, join 2nd leaflet.
Ch of 10 ds, p, 11 ds. Reverse work.
Repeat first leaflet, join first p to 6th r of daisy.
Repeat r, ch 16 ds.
Join first r of daisy to first leaflet and 5th r of first daisy.

28 Valentine Pair *(page 110)*

FINISHED SIZE
Approximately 1 1/4" wide.

MATERIALS
DMC Cordonnet #70 (361-yd. ball): 1 Ecru.

TOOLS AND EQUIPMENT
2 shuttles.

DIRECTIONS
Ch of 5 ds, 3 p sep by 5 ds, 5 ds.
R of 5 ds, 3 p sep by 4 ds, 5 ds, cl r.
R of 5 ds, join to last p of previous r, 4 ds, 2 p sep by 4 ds, 5 ds, cl r. Reverse work.
* Ch of 6 ds.
Small r of 4 ds, join last p of previous r, 5 ds, p, 4 ds, cl r. Reverse work.
Ch of 6 ds.
Large r of 5 ds, join to free p on small r, 5 ds, 4 p sep by 5 ds, 5 ds, cl r.
Largest r of 5 ds, join last p of previous r, 6 p sep by 5 ds, 5 ds, cl r.
Large r of 5 ds, join last p of previous r, 4 p sep by 5 ds, 5 ds, cl r.
Ch of 6 ds.
Small r of 4 ds, join to last p of previous r, 5 ds, p, 4 ds, cl r.
Ch of 6 ds.
R of 5 ds, join to free p on small r, 5 ds, 2 p sep by 5 ds, 5 ds, cl r.
R of 5 ds, join to last p of previous r, 5 ds, 2 p sep by 5 ds, 5 ds, cl r.
Ch of 5 ds, join to last p of previous long ch, 5 ds, 3 p sep by 5 ds, 5 ds, cl r.
R of 5 ds, p, 4 ds, join to 2nd p of previous r, 4 ds, p, 5 ds, cl r.
R of 5 ds, join to last p of previous r, 4 ds, join to free p of 8th r in previous motif, 4 ds, p, 5 ds, cl r.
Repeat from * to desired length.
Crocheted border: Along top edge, work 2 hdc or 2 trc with ch 2 or 3 between, to form a more substantial edge, joining p's on ch's and placing them where long ch's join each other.

THE DELINEATOR

ILLUSTRATING

METROPOLITAN FASHIONS

VOL. XX., No. 1.]   JULY, 1882.   [PRICE. 15 CENTS. OR 8½ PENCE
YEARLY, $1, OR 5s.

SEASONABLE STYLES.

PREVAILING AND INCOMING FASHIONS.

July and August are counted as an intermediate season by the world of Fashion, which ornaments itself in consonance with the raiment Dame Nature is wearing at this time; and hence it is that there are few marked transitions of style in woman's apparel at this period of ornamental accessory articles and fancy that never designs of articles of dress, which, we should remember, are bestowed colors, rather than as devices to which are really entitled.

FASHIONS FOR LADIES.

Although number of patterns published for during this month is the designs are choice and seasonable style, and will be found admirable to fill in disappointing spaces Summer wardrobe handsomely those that for on, were commend

LADIES' Princess front fitted under-arm darts trimmed back, also cut in Princess style, but handsomely adjusted to the figure by a low side-back gore at each side and a broad cluster of graduated shirrings at the waist-line, is suited to any soft goods, either cotton or woolen. It will be in especial favor for fancy-colored, twilled wash silks, foulards and pongees for house dresses that are to form part of a bridal *trousseau*. This style of garment is ordinarily mentioned as a tea gown, because it is sure to be worn in the afternoon, when tea is usually served in the drawing-room or library. In England the service of tea at this hour exists as a fixity, and in America it is becoming a custom, so that no matter whether the lady visits or is visited, she is sure of having her cup of tea. For this most informal of hospitalities, a receiving gown is required that suggests domesticity. The front of such a dress may be overlaid with fancy goods, shirrings or laces, or, perhaps, be decorated with lace *jabots*, ribbon bows with fluttering ends, etc. Its lower edge may be finished with ruffles of the material or lace, plaitings, embroideries or deep flounces, or with any other trimming suited to its material. The pattern has large patch-pockets upon the sides and a high turn-over collar about the neck, and its wrists are prettily and fancifully finished to accord with the other edges. Altogether, it is very elegant in its suggestions.

informal manner. The gores are covered nearly to the belt with shirred and puffed decoration of the material, the lower part of which falls in a deep flounce, a similarly shirred flounce trimming the lower part of the back-breadth. The lower edge of the flounce may trimmed to correspond with the drapery, or may be finished plain as preferred. The jacket waist is finely fitted by bust and under arm darts, under-arm and side-form seams and a center seam. back of the garment is deeper than the remainder, and extra width allowed below the waist-line are laid in three box-plaits underneath. The side-back plaits overlap the center-backs under buttons, stylish effect; and a high and wide rolling collar completes neck. Two rows of braid are usually applied upon the collar, three on the deeper portion of the basque and the front of drapery; and the sleeves and fronts are finished with braid in military fashion. Altogether, this is a stylish pattern for a costume to wear in Midsummer, as well as during any other part of the year.

LADIES' WRAP.—A very handsome style of wrap for cashmere camel's-hair, satin, Surah, pongee, silk-lined Spanish lace or fancy grenadine, is among the shapes for July. It will also be much liked mourning wraps to trim with tape fringes, plaitings of the goods etc. It has a medium-long sack front, which may hang loose being fastened at the throat by a clasp or beneath a ribbon bow which may be closed its depth with buttons, Brandenburgs, fancy loops, etc. The sleeves are of comfortable width and something the mandarin fashion, being parts of the back, which is fitted curved seam and is quite short at the center, extending in long however, at the sides. A ribbon sash is fastened at the center the back, and bows of narrow ribbon are placed upon the lower part of its deep sides. The neck may be completed by ruching the goods, feather bands, or full plaitings of lace. This promises be a favorite fashion with ladies of taste.

LADIES' POLONAISES.—Midsummer emphasizes an earlier assurance that polonaises were to be again as popular as ever. Two attractive designs, just published for these garments, display a pleasing adaptability to mulls and muslins, Surahs and foulards, cotton prints plain sateens, tissues and laces, grenadines and rich silks, and are simple in their construction as they are stylish and attractive their appearance. Such polonaises will be worn with skirts of same or of contrasing fabric. For wash goods, they are especially attractive. One of these has a Princess back, with extra widths laid in plaits underneath below the waist-line. In the center seam of the back drapery a trimmed piece of the goods is inserted

29

(page 111)

FINISHED SIZE
Approximately 5/8" wide.

MATERIALS
DMC Cordonnet #70 (361-yd. ball): 1 Ecru.

TOOLS AND EQUIPMENT
2 shuttles.

DIRECTIONS
R of 4 ds, 3 p sep by 4 ds, 4 ds, cl r.
Ch of 14 ds.

R as above.
Ch of 14 ds.
R of 4 ds, join first p to last p of first r, 2 p sep by 4 ds,
4 ds, cl r.
Ch of 14 ds.
R of 4 ds, join first p to last p of 2nd r, 2 p sep by 4 ds,
4 ds, cl r.
Continue in this same manner to desired length,
joining last ch to base of first r.

30

FINISHED SIZE
Approximately 1 1/4" wide.

MATERIALS
DMC Cebelia #30 (515m ball): 1 White.

TOOLS AND EQUIPMENT
2 shuttles.

DIRECTIONS
Rnd 1: R of 4 ds, 3 p sep by 4 ds, 4 ds, cl r. Reverse
work.
Ch of 4 ds, 3 p sep by 2 ds, 4 ds. Reverse work.
Repeat r, joining first p of new r to last p of previous r.
Continue in this same manner until long enough to
fit around fabric. Join last r to first r. Tie off.
Rnd 2: R of 4 ds, 3 p sep by 4 ds, 4 ds, cl r. Reverse
work.
Ch of 4 ds, p, 4 ds, join to middle p of any ch on rnd
1, 4 ds.

Small r of 4 ds, join to last p of previous r, 4 ds, p, 4 ds,
cl r. Reverse work.
Ch of 4 ds, join to middle p of next ch on previous
rnd, 4 ds, p, 4 ds.
R of 4 ds, join to last p of small r, 4 ds, join to middle p
of first r, 4 ds, p, 4 ds, cl r. Reverse work.
Ch of 4 ds.
R of 4 ds, join to last p of previous r, 4 p sep by 2 ds, 4
ds, cl r.
R of 4 ds, join to last p of previous r, 6 p sep by 2 ds, 4
ds, cl r.
R of 4 ds, join to last p of previous r, 4 p sep by 2 ds, 4
ds, cl r.
Ch of 4 ds.
Start at beginning of rnd 2 and continue in this same
manner around, remembering to join first p of first r
to last p of last r made.

31

FINISHED SIZE
Approximately 7 1/4" diameter.

MATERIALS
DMC Cebelia #30 (249-yd. ball): 1 Tan #619.

TOOLS AND EQUIPMENT
2 shuttles.

DIRECTIONS
Row 1: * R of 2 ds, 5 p sep by 3 ds, 2 ds, cl r. Reverse work.
Ch of 3 ds, 5 p sep by 3 ds, 3 ds. * Reverse work.
Repeat 5 more times, joining 2nd and 4th p's of r's. Tie off.
Row 2: * R of 2 ds, 2 p sep by 3 ds, join to 2nd p of any ch of first row, 2 p sep by 3 ds, 2 ds, cl r. Reverse work.
Ch of 4 ds, 5 p sep by 4 ds, 4 ds. Reverse work. *
Repeat 11 more times, joining 2nd r to 4th p of same ch. Continue around, joining r's to 2nd and 4th p of ch's of row 1. Tie off.
Row 3: * Ch of 4 ds, 2 p sep by 4 ds, join to middle p of any ch of row 2, 4 ds, 2 p sep by 4 ds, 4 ds. Reverse work.
R of 2 ds, 5 p sep by 3 ds, 2 ds, cl r. Reverse work.
* * Ch of 3 ds, 5 p sep by 3 ds, 3 ds. Reverse work.
R of 2 ds, p, 3 ds, join to 4th p of previous r, 3 ds, 3 p sep by 3 ds, 2 ds, cl r. Reverse work. * *
Repeat from * * to * * 4 more times (this forms cluster of r's).
Ch of 4 ds, 2 p sep by 4 ds, join to middle p of next ch of row 2, 4 ds, 2 p sep by 4 ds, 4 ds. Reverse work.
R of 2 ds, p, 3 ds, join to 4th p of last ch between r's in cluster, 3 ds, 3 p sep by 3 ds, p, 2 ds, cl r. * Reverse work.
Repeat from * to * of row 3, 5 more times, joining 2nd p of first ch in cluster of r's to 4th p of single r between clusters. Tie off.

32

FINISHED SIZE
Approximately 5 1/2" diameter.

MATERIALS
Schewe Fil D'Ecosse #16 (400m ball): 1 White #106.
1 5/8" diameter circle of fabric.

TOOLS AND EQUIPMENT
2 shuttles.

DIRECTIONS
* * R of 3 ds, 5 p sep by 4 ds, 3 ds, cl r. Reverse work.
* Ch of 4 ds, 5 p sep by 4 ds, 4 ds. Reverse work.
R of 3 ds, p, 3 ds, join to 4th p of previous r, 3 p sep by 4 ds, 3 ds. *
Repeat from * to * 5 more times, joining 4th p of 7th r to 2nd p of first r. Reverse work.
Ch of 3 ds, 5 p sep by 3 ds, 3 ds. Reverse work.

R of 3 ds, p, 3 ds, join to 2nd p of 6th ch made, 3 ds, 3 p sep by 3 ds, 3 ds, cl r. Reverse work.
Ch of 3 ds, 5 p sep by 3 ds, 3 ds. Reverse work. * *
Repeat from * * to * * 4 more times, joining 4th picot of first ch of each new cluster of r's to 4th p of single r between clusters.
Join threads at beginning. Tie off.
Work buttonhole st around outer edge of fabric piece with crochet thread.
Begin joining p in center of 6 petal design. Join thread with sl st in any buttonhole st, ch 3, dc in next st, ch 2, sc in next p, ch 2, sk next buttonhole st, dc in ea of next 2 sts, ch 2, sc in next p, ch 2, sk next buttonhole st, dc in ea of next 2 sts, * (ch 1, sc in next p, ch 1, sk next buttonhole st, dc in ea of next 2 sts) twice, (ch 2, sc in next p, ch 2, sk next buttonhole st, * * dc in ea of next 2 sts) twice, rep from * around, end last rep at * *, sl st in 3rd ch of beg ch-3. Fasten off.

33

FINISHED SIZE
Approximately 2" wide.

MATERIALS
DMC Cebelia #30 (515m ball): 1 Ecru.

TOOLS AND EQUIPMENT
One shuttle; size #9 crochet hook.

DIRECTIONS
This edging is made in 3 rows with a crocheted top border added to stabilize it. Long p's are used throughout.
Row 1: Lower section: Large r of 6 ds, long p, 2 ds, 3 p sep by 2 ds, 2 ds, long p, 6 ds, cl r.
R of 3 ds.
R of 3 ds, long p, 3 ds, long p, 6 ds, cl r.
R of 3 ds.
Large r as above, joined to previous large r.
R of 3 ds.
R of 6 ds, join to previous smaller r at top p, 3 ds, p, 3 ds, cl r.

R of 3 ds.
Repeat from beginning to desired length. Tie off.
Row 2: Make a 2nd piece just like the first, joining smaller r's in groups of one or 2 to corresponding smaller r's of first section at appropriate long p's. You will be making a mirror image of row 1.
Row 3: R of 3 ds, p, 3 ds, join to center free p of first large r of previous row, 3 ds, p, 3 ds, cl r.
R of 3 ds.
R of 3 ds, 3 p sep by 3 ds, 3 ds, cl r.
R of 3 ds.
Continue across, joining first p of next r to last p of previous r on both rows of r's of 3 ds and 3 p.
To crochet a stable edge across top, sl st into free p of each r across, with ch 3 or 4 between each sl st. Be sure the tension of this row allows work to lie flat. Ch 1, turn. Work 3 or 4 sc in each ch sp of previous row, again making sure work lies flat as this row progresses. Use more or fewer stitches here as needed.

STYLES FOR BOYS

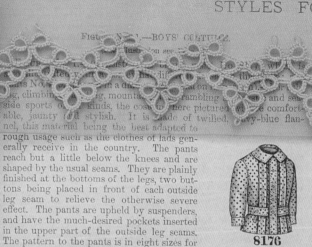

8176   **8176**
Front View.   *Back View.*

BOYS' CAMISOLE.
(For Description see this Page.)

Fig. No. 1.—BOYS' COSTUME.

(For Illustration see this Page.)

... side sports of ... kinds, the costume here pictured ... comfortable, jaunty and stylish. It is made of twilled, navy-blue flannel, this material being the best adapted to rough usage such as the clothes of lads generally receive in the country. The pants reach but a little below the knees and are shaped by the usual seams. They are plainly finished at the bottoms of the legs, two buttons being placed in front of each outside leg seam to relieve the otherwise severe effect. The pants are upheld by suspenders, and have the much-desired pockets inserted in the upper part of the outside leg seams. The pattern to the pants is in eight sizes for boys from three to ten years of age, and costs 7d. or 15 cents.

The blouse is quite *négligé* in appearance, and its lower edge is adjusted to the size of the waist by an elastic band inserted in its wide hem, the blouse drooping over the top of the pants in true sailor fashion. A box-plait is arranged upon the front edge of the left front, and a hem-facing is sewed to the opposite front, two rows of narrow white braid being arranged upon each front just back of these accessories. An ample patch-pocket is machine-stitched to the left front, and a round collar is about the neck; the collar being bordered about its edges with a row of braid. The sleeves are loose, but not at all clumsy, and are gathered at the wrists to braid-trimmed, cuff-like wristbands, which close at the inside of the arm. They are also slightly gathered across the top before they are sewed into the arms'-eyes. The pattern to the waist is in ten sizes for boys from three to twelve years of age, and costs 10d. or 20 cents. It is one of the newest, simplest and most comfortable styles of waists for young lads, and may be like or unlike the pants in material. The same material is, however, preferable to two different kinds in a costume of this style, when both garments are to be of woolen texture. Cambric, linen, lawn, print, etc., are, however, equally suitable for blouses of this description.

The sailor hat is of fine straw, banded about with navy-blue ribbon falling in short ...

... underlapping edge of the front is turned under for a wide hem, and the opposite edge is laid in a box-plait, which is stitched finely about a-quarter of an inch from each edge. In each side, a little back of the closing, is formed a box-plait that is slightly wider, and three similar plaits are folded in the back. All of these plaits are stitched to position underneath, each one being pressed flatly over the sewing, entirely concealing it. These plaits do not, however, perform the entire adjustment, there being a little fullness between and at each side of those in the back, which is taken up in short rows of gathers, the rows being arranged in pairs, one row of each pair being at the waist-line and the other a little more than an inch below. There is also a little fullness back of the box-plait in each side of the front, which is disposed in gathers in the same manner. A narrow belt of the material is stitched at the waist-line, with its upper edge even with the upper rows of gathers and the end at the left side terminating beneath the inner fold of the plait at the closing. Flat buttons are sewed at intervals upon the belt to button the pants upon. The sleeve has a seam at the inside of the arm, but none at the outside, and is sloped ...

... under side of the ... an overlap, which ... edge is finished ... ... has a ... ... with unusual ... ... on, which are ... ... double and then sew ... ... the joinings of all the ... ... The narrow portion ... joined to the neck in an ... which its inner part ... about the neck ... smoothly over ... ... or button-holes and buttons.

Linens, prints, ginghams, flannels, and all materials in use for camisoles or shirt-waists, make up neatly and stylishly in this way. The pieces upon the shoulders prevent the seams beneath from being unduly strained, and the pattern is planned with provision for the wear and tear which healthy boyhood is likely to inflict upon all articles of clothing.

We have pattern No. 8176 in ten sizes for boys from three to twelve years of age. Of material twenty-seven inches wide, two yards and three-eighths will be needed in making a camisole for a boy of seven years. If goods thirty-six inches wide be selected, then a yard and seven-eighths will suffice. Price of pattern, 10d. or 20 cents.

BOYS' BLOUSE WAIST.

(For Illustrations see this Page.)

No. 8177.—This blouse waist, developed in a different material, forms a portion of the jaunty costume represented at Boys' figure No. 1 on page 28.

This blouse is easy to wear and also easy to make, and its shape is particularly adapted to the fabrics in vogue at this time. The front has a narrow box-plait added to its overlapping closing edge ... and hem-facing attached to its opposite ... ... button-holes ... through ...

Front View.   *Back View.*

BOYS' BLOUSE WAIST.

(For Description see this Page.)

... the waist, the ... ... over the casing in regular sailor fashion. The sleeves are each formed of a single section of material and shaped by a seam at the inside of the arm. They are sloped off a little toward the wrist, and the seams are discontinued a short distance from the bottom. The lower edge of each is gathered and sewed between the edges of a double wristband having its corners clipped off diagonally, and the top is lifted over the shoulder by a few gathers before being sewed into the arm's-eye. There is a round collar about the neck, which is rendered shapely, as well as comfortable for Summer wear, by being cut away at the ends so as to flare slightly at each side of the throat. The material represented is mixed flannel, and the collar and wristbands are each trimmed with two rows of braid. A large pocket, with a rounding lower edge, is upon the left front, its upper edge being hemmed and bordered with two straight rows of braid. The seam joining it to the front is also covered with braid.

Linen, duck, gingham and all materials used for boys' blouses make up satisfactorily in this way.

We have pattern No. 8177 in ten sizes for boys from three to ...

34

FINISHED SIZE
Approximately 1 1/8" wide.

MATERIALS
Coats and Clark tatting thread #70 (125-yd. ball): 1 Canary Yellow #10A.

TOOLS AND EQUIPMENT
2 shuttles.

DIRECTIONS
Use 2 shuttles.
Small r of 5 ds, 2 p sep by 5 ds, 5 ds, cl r. Reverse work.
Ch of 9 ds. Reverse work.
Make small r, joining first p to last p of previous r. Reverse work.

Using other shuttle, make small r.
Ch of 9 ds. Reverse work.
Make small r, joining to previous r.
Using same shuttle, make large r of 5 ds, join to previous small r, 5 ds, 2 p sep by 5 ds, 5 ds, cl r.
Using same shuttle, make small r, join first p to last p of large r. Reverse work.
Ch of 9 ds.
Small r, join first p to last p of previous r.
With other shuttle, make small r, joining first p to the 2nd p on the 2nd r from the beginning. Reverse work.
Ch of 9 ds.
Small r, join first p of last r.
Repeat design to desired length, joining first p of r #3 in each group to last p of r #7 from previous group.

35

FINISHED SIZE
Approximately 1 3/8" wide.

MATERIALS
DMC Cordonnet #50 (286-yd. ball): 1 Ecru.

TOOLS AND EQUIPMENT
2 shuttles.

DIRECTIONS
* Large r of 3 ds, 3 p sep by 3 ds, 3 ds, cl r.
Ch of 4 ds.
Small r of 5 ds, p, 5 ds, cl r.
Ch of 4 ds.

Repeat first large r, joining first p of new large r to 3rd p of first large r.
Ch 4.
Small r of 5 ds, join to p of previous small r, 5 ds, cl r.
Ch 4.
Repeat from *. Continue in this same manner to desired length. This forms one half of the double edging.
To turn and complete the 2nd half of edging, ch 12. Then begin again with first r as above. As you progress, join first and 2nd small r's of new section to corresponding first and 2nd small r's of first half of edging.

36

FINISHED SIZE
Approximately 15" across.

MATERIALS
DMC Cordonnet #30 (216m ball): 1 Ecru.

TOOLS AND EQUIPMENT
One shuttle; one ball.

DIRECTIONS
This piece is made almost entirely with just a shuttle thread. Only the borders make use of the chain.

Front or back (make 2): R of 3 ds, 3 p sep by 3 ds, 3 ds, cl r. Leave 1/8" between r's throughout.

Repeat r.

R of 3 ds, join to last p of first r, 3 ds, 2 p sep by 3 ds, 3 ds, cl r.

R of 3 ds, join to last p of 2nd r, 3 ds, 2 p sep by 3 ds, 3 ds, cl r.

Continue alternating in this same manner, until you have a double row of r's 15" long. Tie off.

Make a 2nd double row of r's, joining it to the free p's along one edge of the first double row.

Make a 3rd double row of r's, joining it to the 2nd double row.

Sleeve (make 2): The sleeve piece on each side connects front to back, forming a simple rectangle. It is made of 2 double rows of r's. The sleeve on the model piece is approximately 6" long.

Begin first double row of sleeve piece by joining first p of new r to free p of 2nd r from end of front. Work new double row for 6", joining last p of last r to first free p of 2nd r from end of back.

Work a 2nd double row in this same manner, joining it to the first double row in the same manner for the front and back, connecting beginning and end of row to front and back, joining at 4th and 5th r's of front and back on both sides.

Repeat for 2nd sleeve.

Border (worked around neckline and outside edge of sleeve): Ch of 3 ds, 3 p sep by 1 ds, 3 ds.

R of 3 ds, p, 3 ds, join to any free p on neckline (except for the first or last p on any side).

Continue around neckline, alternating r's and ch's, being sure to join r's to each other as you work.

Important note: To form the inside corner as you work around, join the last free p of one side and the first free p of next side by the same new ring.

Work the same border across outside edge of each sleeve, starting and ending with the last free p of that edge.

Weave a drawstring through where border meets top double row of neckline.

37

FINISHED SIZE
Center front approximately 6".

MATERIALS
DMC Cordonnet #50 (286-yd. ball): 1 Ecru.

TOOLS AND EQUIPMENT
One shuttle; one ball.

DIRECTIONS
This yoke is made entirely with a shuttle, except for a ch to stabilize the ends of both pieces.

Simple flower: R of 5 ds, 3 p sep by 5 ds, 5 ds, cl r.
* R of 5 ds, join to last p of first r, 5 ds, 2 p sep by 5 ds, 5 ds, cl r. *
Repeat from * to * 2 more times, being sure to join last p of 4th r to first p of first r. Tie off.
To join flower, join 2nd p of first new r of next flower to any free p of previous flower, continue to make the simple flower. Join next flower to previous ones directly opposite the previous joining forming a straight line.
Make 2 separate rows (one for front, one for back) of 23 flowers each.

Front: Make one row of 9 flowers, joined at the 8th flower of row 23.
Make one row of 7 flowers, joined to the 2nd flower of the row of 9 flowers.
Make one row of 5 flowers, joined to the 2nd flower of the row of 7 flowers.
Make one row of 3 flowers, joined to the 2nd flower of the row of 5 flowers.
Make one flower, connected to the center flower of the row of 3 flowers.
Along the edge of free p's of row of 23 flowers, with shuttle only, work large r of 6 ds, 3 p sep by 6 ds, 6 ds. cl r. Leave 3/8" between all r's on this row.
Small r of 6 ds, p, 6 ds, cl r.
Large r as above, joining to previous large r and free p of top of first flower.
Continue in this same manner, alternating large and small r's, joining every other large r to a flower across. This double row now becomes the top of the front piece.

Back: Work a matching double row across one edge of row of 23 flowers for back. This becomes the top of the back piece.
The bottom of the back piece is a double row of only large r's as follows:
large r of 6 ds, 3 p sep by 6 ds, 6 ds, cl r. Reverse work. Leave 1/8" between all large r's on this row. Make another large r.
Large r, joined to first large r and first free p of lower edge of flower row.
Large r, joined to 2nd large r.
Continue across, joining every other large r on one side of row to a flower.
The bottom front is made in this same manner.
Be sure as you work around the v-shape of the front piece, that you join this double row of large r's to both free p's of each flower you come to. At the point of the v at center front, work a cluster of 3 large r's, joined to each other on the free edge of double row.
To connect the front to the back and to form the shoulder straps, work one continuous double row around top edge as follows:
Beginning at left side of back, work small r of 6 ds, join to free p of first small r of top row of back, 6 ds, cl r. Reverse work.
Large r of 5 ds, 5 p sep by 3 ds, 5 ds, cl r.
Repeat across back, joining large r's to each other and small r's to existing top row. Do not tie off, but continue this double row for 11" to form the shoulder strap. Continue across front, same as for back and form 2nd shoulder strap. Tie off.
A ch of (4 ds, p) may be worked along ends of yoke and along small r side of shoulder strap to stabilize.
The model is stitched to fine netting to give it more body.

38

FINISHED SIZE
Approximately 7 1/2" diameter.

MATERIALS
Schewe Fil D'Ecosse #16 (400m ball): 1 Beige #115.

TOOLS AND EQUIPMENT
2 shuttles.

DIRECTIONS
Center: R of 2 ds, 12 p sep by 2 ds, 2 ds, cl r. Tie off.
Row 1: Ch of 8 ds, join a p on center, 8 ds. Reverse work.
* R of 2 ds, 5 p sep by 2 ds, 2 ds, cl r. Reverse work. Ch of 8 ds, skip 1 p and join next on center r, 8 ds. Reverse work. *
Repeat from * to * 4 more times, making 1 more r at end of row. Tie off.

Row 2: Ch of 3 ds, 13 p sep by 1 ds, 3 ds, join to middle p of r on row 1 and repeat ch 5 more times. Join. Tie off.
Row 3: Ch of 7 ds.
* R of 7 ds, join 3rd p of any ch on row 1, 7 ds, cl r. Ch of 7 ds.
R of 2 ds, 5 p sep by 2 ds, 2 ds, cl r.
Ch of 7 ds. *
Repeat from * to *, joining the 7th and 11th p of same ch, ultimately joining the 3rd, 7th and 11th p of each ch of row 2. Join. Tie off.
Row 4: Ch of 3 ds, 9 p sep by 1 ds, 3 ds, join middle p of r's on row 3. Repeat around. Join. Tie off.
Row 5: * Ch of 2 ds, 13 p sep by 1 ds, 2 ds. Reverse work.
R of 7 ds, join 5th p of ch in row 4, 7 ds, cl r. Reverse work. *
Repeat from * to * around. Join. Tie off.

39

FINISHED SIZE
Approximately 3 3/4" wide.

MATERIALS
Schewe Fil D'Ecosse #16 (400m ball): 1 Wheat #155.

TOOLS AND EQUIPMENT
2 shuttles.

DIRECTIONS
COLLAR
Note: Make long p's throughout.
Motif (make 9): **Rnd 1:** R of 8 ds, p, 8 ds, cl r. Reverse work.
* Ch of 4 ds, 5 p sep by 2 ds, 4 ds. Reverse work.
R of 8 ds, join to p of first r, 8 ds, cl r. *
Repeat from * to * 3 more times.
Repeat ch one more time. Join. Tie off.
Rnd 2: R of 8 ds, join to last p of any ch of previous rnd, 8 ds, cl r.

Ch of 4 ds, 5 p sep by 2 ds, 4 ds.
Repeat r's and ch's around, joining r's to first, 3rd and 5th p's of rnd 1. There will be 15 repeats around. Join. Tie off.
To connect motifs to each other, join 2 or 3 adjacent p's of corresponding ch sections to form a row of 9 motifs. This row is the lower section of the collar.
Top section: R of 8 ds, p, 8 ds, cl r.
Ch of 4 ds, join to last p of 4th ch section from where motif #1 joins motif #2, 2 ds, join next p, 3 p sep by 2 ds, 4 ds.
* R of 8 ds, join to first r, 8 ds, cl r.
Ch of 4 ds, 5 p sep by 2 ds, 5 ds. *
Repeat from * to * 2 more times.
Repeat r once. Reverse work.
Ch of 4 ds, skipping one whole section of ch of previous rnd, join first p of next ch section, 2 ds, join to next p of same section of ch, 8 p sep by 2 ds, 4 ds.
Repeat from beginning of top section, joining each motif in the same manner as the first one.

40

FINISHED SIZE
Approximately 8 1/4" diameter.

MATERIALS
DMC Cebelia #30 (515m ball): 1 Tan #619.

TOOLS AND EQUIPMENT
2 shuttles.

DIRECTIONS
Row 1: * R of 8 ds, large p, 8 ds, cl r. Reverse work.
Ch 8, 3 p sep by 4 ds, 8 ds. Reverse work. *
Repeat from * to * 5 more times, joining each r to
large p of first r. Tie off.
Row 2: * Ch of 3 ds, 3 p sep by 3 ds, 3 ds.
R of 2 ds, 5 p sep by 2 ds, 2 ds, cl r. Reverse work.
Ch of 3 ds, p, 3 ds, join to any middle p of ch of row
1, 3 ds, p, 3 ds. Reverse work.
R of 2 ds, 5 p sep by 2 ds, 2 ds. Reverse work. *
Repeat from * to * 5 more times.
Row 3: * Ch of 10 ds. Reverse work.

R of 2 ds, 2 p sep by 2 ds, 2 ds, join to middle p of r of
row 2, 2 ds, 2 p sep by 2 ds, 2 ds, cl r. Reverse work.
Ch of 10 ds. Reverse work.
R of 2 ds, 7 p sep by 2 ds, 2 ds, cl r. Reverse work. *
Repeat from * to * 11 more times.
Row 4: * R of 2 ds, p, 2 ds, join to 6th p of r of row 3, 2
ds, 5 p sep by 2 ds, 2 ds, cl r. Reverse work.
Ch of 3 ds, 3 p sep by 3 ds, 3 ds. Reverse work.
R of 2 ds, p, 2 ds, join to 6th p of previous r, 2 ds, 5 p
sep by 2 ds, 2 ds, cl r. Reverse work.
Ch of 3 ds, 3 p sep by 3 ds, 3 ds. Reverse work.
R of 2 ds, p, 2 ds, join to 6th p of previous r, 2 ds, 3 p
sep by 2 ds, 2 ds, join to 2nd p of next r of row 3, 2 ds,
p, 2 ds, cl r. Reverse work.
Ch of 3 ds, 3 p sep by 3 ds, 3 ds. Reverse work. *
Repeat from * to * 11 more times.
Row 5: * R of 2 ds, 3 p sep by 2 ds, 2 ds, join to middle
p of any ch of row 4, 2 ds, 3 p sep by 2 ds, 2 ds, cl r.
Reverse work.
Ch of 3 ds, 3 p sep by 3 ds, 3 ds. *
Repeat from * to * around.

41

FINISHED SIZE
Approximately 3 3/4" wide.

MATERIALS
Schewe Fil D'Ecosse #16 (400m ball): 1 Beige #115.

TOOLS AND EQUIPMENT
2 shuttles.

DIRECTIONS
Large motif (made up of 5 small motifs): R of 5 ds, p, 5 ds, cl r.

Ch of 6 ds.

R of 5 ds, p, 5 ds, cl r. Reverse work.

Ch of 4 ds, 2 p sep by 4 ds, 4 ds.

* R of 5 ds, join to p of r just made, 5 ds, cl r. Reverse work.

Ch of 4 ds, 2 p sep by 4 ds, 4 ds.

R of 5 ds, join to same p as other 2 r's, 5 ds, cl r. Reverse work.

Ch of 4 ds, 2 p sep by 4 ds, 4 ds.

R of 5 ds, join to same p as others, 5 ds, cl r. Reverse work.

Ch of 4 ds, 2 p sep by 4 ds, 4 ds.

R of 5 ds, join to same p as other, 5 ds, cl r. Reverse work.

Ch of 6 ds.

R of 5 ds, join to p of very first r made, 5 ds, cl r. Reverse work.

Ch of 6 ds.

R of 5 ds, p, 5 ds, cl r. Reverse work.

Ch of 4 ds, join to last p of 4th ch of previous small motif, 4 ds, p, 4 ds. *

Repeat from * to * 4 more times, joining last p of 4th ch of 5th small motif to first p of first ch of first small motif. Join. Tie off.

After making the first large motif, start the 2nd motif in the same manner, joining the 2nd p of the 2nd ch of the new small motif to any first p of 2nd ch of any small motif in large motif, and continue to make 2nd large motif same as the first.

The 3rd and remaining large motifs will be joined in the same manner, going clockwise from previous joining, skipping one small motif and joining at the next small motif. Be sure each joining is at the corresponding place on each large motif to form a straight line of large motifs.

The remaining 2 small motifs of the large motif that are side by side will be used for joining large motif to the top band.

Make as many large motifs as desired.

After desired number of large motifs are completed and joined together, the top band is made in 2 rows as follows:

Row 1: + Ch of 6 ds.

R of 5 ds, p, 5 ds, cl r.

* Ch of 4 ds, 2 p sep by 4 ds, 4 ds.

R of 5 ds, join to previous r, 5 ds, cl r. *

Ch of 4 ds, join to first p of corresponding ch of top small motif of first large motif, 4 ds, join to next p, 4 ds.

R of 5 ds, join to p of previous r, 5 ds, cl r. Reverse work.

Repeat from * to * once.

Ch of 6 ds.

R of 5 ds, p, 5 ds, cl r.

Repeat from +, joining first p of each first ch to last p of 3rd ch of previous small motif.

Join 2 large motifs to band, then make small motif and do not join anything to it, join 2 large motifs to band, make small motif and do not join anything to it, etc., end with ch of 6 ds.

R of 5 ds, p, 5 ds, cl r. Tie off.

Row 2: R of 5 ds, join to last free r, 5 ds, cl r.

* Ch of 4 ds, p, 4 ds.

R of 5 ds, join to same place as last joining, 5 ds, cl r. *

Repeat from * to * 2 more times.

Ch of 6 ds.

R of 5 ds, join to group of 4 r's of previous row, 5 ds, cl r. Reverse work.

Ch of 6 ds.

R of 5 ds, join to next free r, 5 ds, cl r.

Ch of 4 ds, join to previous corresponding ch, 4 ds.

Continue in this same manner across.

FINISHED SIZE
Approximately 6" diameter.

MATERIALS
Schewe Fil D'Ecosse #16 (400m ball): 1 Tan #138.

TOOLS AND EQUIPMENT
One shuttle; one ball; size #10 crochet hook.

DIRECTIONS
Note: In all but the very last rnd, p's should be quite small.

Center: Large r of 5 ds, 8 p sep by 5 ds, 5 ds, cl r. Tie off.

Rnd 1: + Ch of 4 ds, 16 p sep by 1 ds, 4 ds.
* R of 9 ds, p, 9 ds, cl r. *
R of 11 ds, join to last p of center r, 11 ds, cl r.
Repeat from * to * once.
Ch of 4 ds, join to last p of previous ch, 1 ds, 15 p sep by 1 ds, 4 ds.
R of 1 ds, join to p of previous r, 10 ds, join to next p of center r, 10 ds, p, 1 ds, cl r.
Repeat from + around 3 more times, joining last single r to base of center r. Tie off.
With crochet hook, work one sc in each free p around, beginning and ending this rnd at center of any group of p's, sl st to join. * Ch 10, sl st to center of next sc section. Repeat from * around. Join. Tie off.

Rnd 2: * R of 10 ds, p, 10 ds, cl r.
Ch of 3 ds, 15 p sep by 1 ds, 3 ds. Join with shuttle thread to p of first r.
R of 2 ds, 3 p sep by 1 ds, 2 ds, p, 10 ds, cl r. Reverse work.
Ch of 10 ds, join to any crochet ch st of previous rnd, 10 ds. Join with shuttle thread to last p of previous r.
Repeat from * around, skipping 5 or 6 crochet ch sts between joinings. Tie off.
Work sc border around this section, being sure to work one sc in each free p of alternating r's and ch's, and remembering to begin at center of tatted ch section. Sl st to join. * Ch 11, sl st to center of next sc section. Repeat from * around. Join. Tie off.

Rnd 3: R of 5 ds, p, 4 ds, p, 5 ds, cl r.
Ch of 7 ds, p, 5 ds.
* R of 5 ds, join to 2nd p of last r, 4 ds, p, 5 ds, cl r. *
+ Ch of 5 ds, p, 5 ds, p, 1 ds, p, 5 ds. +
Repeat from * to *.
Ch of 3 ds, 5 p sep by 1 ds, 3 ds.
Repeat last r and ch again.
Repeat from * to *.
Repeat from + to +.
Repeat from * to *.
Ch of 5 ds, p, 7 ds. Reverse work.
Repeat from * to *, joining first p to last r and 2nd p to first p of first r made. Reverse work.
Ch of 7 ds, join to any ch of crocheted ch rnd, 5 ds. Reverse work.
R of 5 ds, join to free p of next to last tatted ch section, 4 ds, p, 5 ds, cl r.
Ch of 5 ds, join to crocheted ch section of previous rnd (skipping 7 ch sts), 7 ds.
R of 5 ds, p, 4 ds, p, 5 ds, cl r.
Ch of 7 ds, join to free p of previous r, 5 ds.
Repeat from * around. Repeat rest of row 13 more times.

43

FINISHED SIZE
Approximately 5 3/4" diameter.

MATERIALS
DMC Cebelia #30 (515m ball): 1 Ecru.

TOOLS AND EQUIPMENT
2 shuttles.

DIRECTIONS
Center: R of 2 ds, 10 p sep by 2 ds, 2 ds, cl r. Tie off.
Row 1: * R of 2 ds, 2 p sep by 2 ds, 2 ds, join to any p on center r, 2 ds, 2 p sep by 2 ds, 2 ds, cl r. Reverse work.
Ch of 3 ds, 3 p sep by 3 ds, 3 ds. Reverse work.
R of 5 ds, join to 5th p of last r, 5 ds, cl r.
Using same shuttle, r of 5 ds, p, 5 ds, cl r. Reverse work.
Ch of 3 ds, 3 p sep by 3 ds, 3 ds. Reverse work. *
Repeat from * to * 4 more times, joining p of next r to p at top of small r. Join threads at beginning of row. Tie off.
Row 2: Clover leaf (make 5 with one shuttle, join to previous row so clover leaf is over 2 small r's): r of 6 ds, join to 2nd p of first ch on previous row, 2 ds, 6 p sep by 2 ds, 3 ds, cl r.

R of 3 ds, join to last p of previous r, 10 p sep by 2 ds, 3 ds, cl r.
R of 3 ds, join to last p of previous r, 2 ds, 5 p sep by 2 ds, 2 ds, join to 2nd p of next ch on previous r, 6 ds, cl r. Join. Tie off.
Row 3: * R of 2 ds, 3 p sep by 2 ds, 2 ds, join to middle p of middle r of clover leaf, 2 ds, 3 p sep by 2 ds, 2 ds, cl r. Reverse work.
Ch of 5 ds, 5 p sep by 3 ds, 5 ds. Reverse work.
R of 2 ds, 3 p sep by 2 ds, 2 ds, join to 6th p of previous r, 2 ds, 3 p sep by 2 ds, 2 ds, cl r.
Using same shuttle, r, repeat same r. Reverse work.
Ch of 5 ds, 5 p sep by 3 ds, 5 ds. Reverse work. *
Repeat from * to *, except do not join first r to a clover leaf but make a r of 2 ds, p, 2 ds, join middle p of last r, 2 ds, 5 p sep by 2 ds, 2 ds, cl r. * *
Repeat from * to * * 4 more times, joining to each clover leaf around.
Row 4: R of 2 ds, 3 p sep by 2 ds, 2 ds, join to 2nd p of ch on previous r, 2 ds, 3 p sep by 2 ds, 2 ds, cl r. Reverse work.
Ch of 3 ds, 5 p sep by 3 ds, 3 ds.
Repeat r's and ch's, join 2nd r to 4th p of same ch. Repeat from beginning of row 4, joining 2nd and 4th p of each ch. Join threads at beginning of row. Tie off.

44

FINISHED SIZE
Approximately 1 3/4" wide.

MATERIALS
DMC Six Cord Brilliant tatting cotton #70 (106-yd. ball): 1 each Rose #604, Ecru.

TOOLS AND EQUIPMENT
One shuttle.

DIRECTIONS
Note: R's have rather large p's.

* R of 3 ds, 5 p sep by 3 ds, 3 ds, cl r. Reverse work.
Ch of 7 ds.
R of 3 ds, 5 p sep by 3 ds, 3 ds.
Ch of 3 ds, 3 p sep by 7 ds, 3 ds, join to center p of previous r.
Ch of 7 ds.
Repeat from * across to desired length. Tie off. This will give you half of the insert.
Work an identical piece, joining center p's of free r as you work. This forms the mirror image 2nd half of the insert.

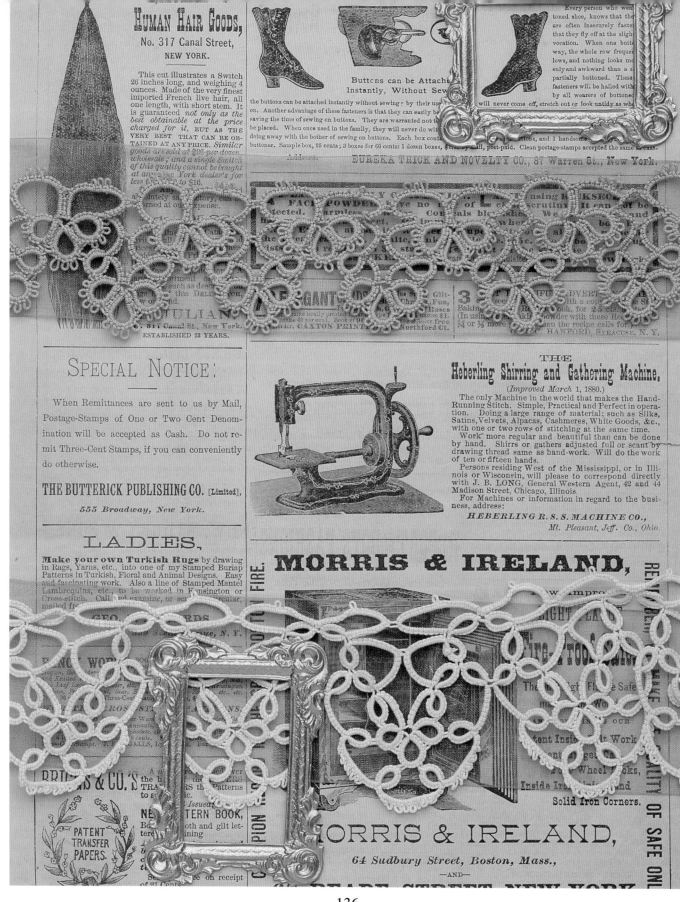

45

FINISHED SIZE
Approximately 1 3/4" wide.

MATERIALS
DMC Cordonnet #40 (249-yd. ball): 1 Ecru.

TOOLS AND EQUIPMENT
2 shuttles.

DIRECTIONS
Clover leaf: * Large r of 6 ds, 6 p sep by 2 ds, 6 ds, cl r. Repeat large r twice more, joining first p of each new r to last p of previous r. Reverse work.
Long ch of 6 ds, p, 5 ds, 3 p sep by 2 ds, 5 ds, p, 6 ds, join to last p of 3rd large r, ch of 6 ds, p, 6 ds. Reverse work.

Small r of 5 ds, join to last p of middle large r, 5 ds, p, 5 ds, cl r.
Ch of 6 ds.
Repeat clover leaf, joining first p of first large r to last p of previous small r.
Ch of 6 ds.
Small r of 5 ds, join to last p of 3rd large r, 5 ds, p, 5 ds, cl r.
Ch of 6 ds, join to p of earlier ch that was made of ch 6, p, ch 6, ch of 6 ds, p, ch of 6 ds, join to last free p of first long ch, 5 ds, 3 p sep by 2 ds, 5 ds, p, 6 ds. Repeat from * with these additions: join first p of first large r to p on remaining ch between clover leaves; join 2nd p of middle r to 2nd p of small r, join first p of first ch 6 to last p of ch just before clover leaf.

46

FINISHED SIZE
Approximately 2 3/8" wide.

MATERIALS
Schewe Fil D'Ecosse #16 (400m ball): 1 Ecru #164.

TOOLS AND EQUIPMENT
One shuttle; one ball.

DIRECTIONS
Rnd 1: Ch of 10 ds, p, 10 ds, p, 10 ds (chain A).
R of 8 ds, p, 8 ds, cl r.
+ Using same shuttle, repeat r.
Ch of 10 ds, p, 9 ds (chain B).
R of 8 ds, join to p of 2nd r, 8 ds, cl r.
Using same shuttle, r of 8 ds, p, 8 ds, cl r.
Ch of 9 ds.
* R of 4 ds, join to p of previous r, 4 ds, 2 p sep by 4 ds, 4 ds, cl r. *
Large r of 5 ds, join to last p of previous r, 4 ds, p, 4 ds, p, 4 ds, p, 5 ds, cl r.
Repeat from * to * once.
Ch of 9 ds.
* * R of 8 ds, join to last p of previous r, 8 ds, cl r. * *
R of 8 ds, p, 8 ds, cl r.

Ch of 9 ds, join to p of chain B above, ch of 10 ds.
Repeat from * * to * * once.
R of 8 ds, p, 8 ds, cl r.
Ch of 10 ds, join to last p of chain A, 10 ds, p, 10 ds, join to p of last r made.
Repeat chain A.
Repeat first r, joining to previous r.
Repeat from + to desired circumference. Join.
Rnd 2: R of 7 ds, join where r's #2 and #3 of previous rnd are joined, 7 ds, cl r.
Ch of 9 ds.
R of 7 ds, join to free p of r #5 of previous rnd, 7 ds, cl r.
Ch of 3 ds, 6 p sep by 2 ds, 3 ds.
R of 7 ds, join to first free p of large r of previous rnd, 7 ds, cl r.
Ch of 3 ds, 8 p sep by 2 ds, 3 ds.
R of 7 ds, join to 2nd free p of same large r, 7 ds, cl r.
Ch of 3 ds, 6 p sep by 2 ds, 3 ds.
R of 7 ds, join p of 7th r of previous rnd, 7 ds, cl r.
Ch of 9 ds.
R of 7 ds, join to p where r's #9 and #10 of previous rnd are joined.
Repeat from beginning of rnd.

47

FINISHED SIZE
Approximately 4" square.

MATERIALS
DMC Cordonnet #20 (174-yd. ball) 1 Ecru.

TOOLS AND EQUIPMENT
2 shuttles.

DIRECTIONS
Begin by making a loop of thread about 1/4" in diameter. This becomes the center of the motif to which you join rnd 1. Tie off.
Rnd 1: * Small r of 4 ds, join to central loop, 4 ds, cl r. Ch of 7 ds.
Large r of 5 ds, 3 p sep by 5 ds, 5 ds, cl r.
Ch of 7 ds.
Repeat from * 11 times, joining first and 3rd p's on side of large r as you work. Finish rnd with ch 7, join to base of first small r. Tie off.
Rnd 2: Clover leaf: Large r of 5 ds, 3 p sep by 5 ds, 5 ds, cl r. * * Large r of 5 ds, join to last p of previous r, 5 ds, join to middle p on any large r of previous rnd, 5 ds, p, 5 ds, cl r.
Large r of 5 ds, join to last p of previous r, 5 ds, 2 p sep by 5 ds, 5 ds, cl r. * * Reverse work.
Ch of 5 ds, 2 p sep by 5 ds, 5 ds. Reverse work.
Large r of 5 ds, join to middle p of previous r, 5 ds, join to free p of next large r of rnd 1, 5 ds, p, 5 ds, cl r. Reverse work.
Ch of 5 ds, 2 p sep by 5 ds, 5 ds. Reverse work.
Large r of 5 ds, join to last p of previous r, 5 ds, join to free p of next large r of rnd 1, 5 ds, p, 5 ds, cl r. Reverse work.
Ch of 5 ds, 2 p sep by 5 ds, 5 ds. Reverse work.
Large r of 5 ds, p, 5 ds, join to last p of previous r, 5 ds, p, 5 ds, cl r.
Repeat from * * to * * once. Reverse work.
Long ch of 6 ds, 6 p sep by 6 ds, 6 ds. One side of square is now complete.
Repeat from beginning of rnd 2, 3 more times, joining 2nd p of first r to 2nd p of 3rd large r of last clover leaf and joining 2nd p of 2nd large r to same p on first row as 2nd large r of previous clover leaf (this forms the corner of the motif). Join at base of first r.

48

FINISHED SIZE
Approximately 5 1/2" diameter.

MATERIALS
DMC Cordonnet #40 (249-yd. ball): 1 Ecru.

TOOLS AND EQUIPMENT
2 shuttles.

DIRECTIONS
Row 1: * R of 5 ds, large p, 5 ds, cl r. Reverse work. Ch of 3 ds, 3 p sep by 3 ds, 3 ds. Reverse work. *
Repeat from * to * 5 more times, joining each new r to p of previous r. Join threads at beginning of row. Tie off.
Row 2: R of 5 ds, join to first p of any ch on previous row, 5 ds, cl r. Reverse work.
Ch of 3 ds, 3 p sep by 3 ds, 3 ds. Reverse work.
Repeat r's and ch's, joining r's to first and 3rd p of each ch of previous row. Join threads at beginning of row. Tie off
Row 3: R of 3 ds, p, 3 ds, join to first p of any ch, 3 ds, p, 3 ds, cl r. Reverse work.
Ch of 3 ds, 3 p sep by 3 ds, 3 ds. Reverse work.
Repeat r's and ch's around, joining first p of next r to 3rd p of last r and 2nd p of r's to first and 3rd p on ch's of previous row. Join threads at beginning of row. Tie off.
Row 4: R of 5 ds, join to middle p of any ch from previous row, 5 ds, cl r. Reverse work.
Ch of 3 ds, 5 p sep by 3 ds, 3 ds. Reverse work.
Repeat r's and ch's around. Join thread at beginning of row. Tie off.
Row 5: R of 3 ds, p, 3 ds, join to 2nd p of any ch of previous row, 3 ds, p, 3 ds, cl r. Reverse work.
Ch of 2 ds, 3 p sep by 2 ds, 2 ds. Reverse work.
Repeat r's and ch's joining first p of new r's to previous r and 2nd p to previous row, joining the 2nd and 4th p of each ch on previous row. Join threads at beginning of row. Tie off.

49

FINISHED SIZE
Approximately 1 1/8" wide.

MATERIALS
Coats and Clark tatting thread #70 (125-yd. ball) 1 Shaded Yellow #19.

TOOLS AND EQUIPMENT
2 shuttles.

DIRECTIONS
Large r of 5 ds, 5 p sep by 4 ds, 5 ds, cl r.
* * Repeat r twice more, joining first p of each new r to last p of previous r.
Ch of 4 ds, p, 4 ds.
Small r of 5 ds, join to 4th p of 3rd large r, 4 ds, p, 4 ds, p, 4 ds, cl r.
Ch of 4 ds, p, 4 ds.
Repeat small r, joining first p to last p of previous r.
Ch of 4 ds, 3 p sep by 4 ds, 4 ds.
* Repeat small r again, joining 2nd p to 2nd p of previous r.
* Ch of 4 ds, p, 4 ds.
Repeat from * to *, joining 2nd p to free p of 4th r previously made.
Ch of 4 ds, p, 4 ds.
Large r, joining 2nd p to last p of previous small r and 3rd p to 3rd large r previously made.
Repeat entire pattern from * *, joining p's of 4 ds chs.
Repeat to desired length.

50

FINISHED SIZE
Approximately 1" wide.

MATERIALS
DMC Cordonnet #40 (249-yd. ball): 1 Ecru.

TOOLS AND EQUIPMENT
2 shuttles.

DIRECTIONS
* R of 3 ds, 3 p sep by 3 ds, 3 ds, cl r. Reverse work.
Ch of 2 ds, 8 p sep by 2 ds, 2 ds. Reverse work.
R of 3 ds, p, 3 ds, join to middle p of first r, 3 ds, p, 3 ds, cl r. Reverse work.
Long ch of 2 ds, 8 p sep by 2 ds, 2 ds. Reverse work.
R of 3 ds, p, 3 ds, join middle p of first r, 3 ds, p, 3 ds, cl r. Reverse work.
Ch of 4 ds, p, 4 ds. Reverse work.
R of 4 ds, join to 7th p of previous long ch, 4 ds, 2 p sep by 4 ds, 4 ds, cl r. Reverse work.
Ch of 4 ds, p, 4 ds. Reverse work.
Repeat from *, joining 2nd p of first long ch to last p of 4 ds-r, to desired length.
The 2nd half is made in this same manner, joining the last 2 p's of the first long ch and the first 2 p's of the 2nd long ch to corresponding p's on the first half of lace.

Rose Buds & Border *(Continued from page 71)*

Large ring: Slide 12 beads up on string. Make ring as close as possible to last join. Ring of 2 ds, 6 beads separated by 1 p, 2 ds, p, 2 ds, 6 beads separated by 1 p, 2 ds. Close. Slide 4 beads up next to ring and join to center picot with shuttle thread.

5th ring: Slide 6 beads up on string. 2 ds, 3 beads separated by 1 p, 2 ds, p, 2 ds, 3 beads separated by 1 p, 2 ds. Close. Slide 2 beads up next to ring and then join to center picot. There are 27 double r's. Tie off. Skip one blue strip and repeat from *. Make a total of 4 red strips.

Make 3 separate long red strips of 47 double r's.

White stripes: Hand stitch lace to red strips and blue area by p's.

Stars: R 3ds, 5p sep by 3ds, 3ds, cl r tie off. Make 50 stars. Glue to blue area (alternate rows of 6 stars and 5 stars) and glue 1 button on top of each star. Insert straight stick on left side of flag, weaving under and over the 1/4" threads.

FINISHED SIZE
Approximately 2 3/4" wide.

MATERIALS
Schewe Fil D'Ecosse #16 (400m ball): 1 each Salmon #142, Light Olive #140.
Mill Hill Antique Glass Beads, 1 package each #03030 and #00275.

TOOLS AND EQUIPMENT
2 shuttles.

DIRECTIONS
First motif: R of 2 ds, 12 p sep by 2 ds, 2 ds, cl r. Tie off.
Row 1: R of 6 ds, join to first p of previous r, 6 ds, cl r. Reverse work. Leave 1/4" thread after all r's.
R of 4 ds, 7 p sep by 2 ds, 4 ds, cl r. Reverse work.
* R of 6 ds, join to next p of first r, 6 ds, cl r. Reverse work.
R of 4 ds, join to last p of large r, 2 ds, 6 p sep by 2 ds, 4 ds, cl r. Reverse work.
Repeat from * around. On last large r, join last p to first p of first r. Tie off.
2nd motif: Work in same manner as for first motif, except first large r is made as follows: r of 4 ds, 3 p sep by 2 ds, 2 ds, join to middle p of any large r of previous motif, 2 ds, 3 p sep by 2 ds, 4 ds, cl r.
Repeat for 2nd large r, joining 4th p of large r to middle p of next large r of first motif.

When joining motifs for straight edge, be sure joinings are opposite each other. There will be 4 free large r's on each side of joinings. For corners, leave only one free large r between joinings.

Edging: R of 3 ds, 7 p sep by 2 ds, 3 ds, cl r.
R of 5 ds, join to last p of previous r, 2 ds, 3 p sep by 2 ds, 2 ds, join to first r after the 2 r's that joined motifs, 2 ds, 4 p sep by 2 ds, 4 ds, cl r.
R of 4 ds, join to last p of previous r, 6 p sep by 2 ds, 4 ds, cl r. Reverse work.
* Ch of 4 ds, 11 p sep by 2 ds, 4 ds. Reverse work.
Clover leaf: R of 3 ds, 3 p sep by 2 ds, join to 4th p of last r, 2 ds, 3 p sep by 2 ds, 4 ds, cl r.
R of 5 ds, join to last p of previous r, 2 ds, 3 p sep by 2 ds, sk 1 r of motif and join to middle p of next motif r, 2 ds, 4 p sep by 2 ds, 4 ds, cl r.
R of 4 ds, join to last p of previous r, 6 p sep by 2 ds, 4 ds, cl r. Reverse work.
Sk one r on motif and join next clover leaf in the same manner.
Between every 2nd and 3rd motif, make a single clover leaf that is not joined to motifs in center.
Repeat from * to desired length. Repeat on opposite side of motifs.
Make motif for corner in the same manner as the others. Make the next motif in the same manner also, except skip only one r, then join in the usual manner.
Corner outside edging: Continue working edging in the same manner, except after making first clover leaf on corner, skip one r, then make 3 clover leaves joining the next 3 r's, skip one more r, make one more clover leaf and then continue as before.
Corner inside edging: After making 2nd clover leaf of last motif before corner, ch of 4 ds, 6 p sep by 2 ds, 4 ds.
Make clover leaf as before, joining to corner motif in r that was skipped.
Repeat above ch, then continue edging as usual, joining clover leaf to next free r on next motif.

142

Metric Conversion Chart

MM - Millimeters   CM - Centimeters
INCHES TO MILLIMETERS AND CENTIMETERS

INCHES	MM	CM	INCHES	CM	INCHES	CM
⅛	3	0.3	9	22.9	30	76.2
¼	6	0.6	10	25.4	31	78.7
⅜	10	1.0	11	27.9	32	81.3
½	13	1.3	12	30.5	33	83.8
⅝	16	1.6	13	33.0	34	86.4
¾	19	1.9	14	35.6	35	88.9
⅞	22	2.2	15	38.1	36	91.4
1	25	2.5	16	40.6	37	94.0
1¼	32	3.2	17	43.2	38	96.5
1½	38	3.8	18	45.7	39	99.1
1¾	44	4.4	19	48.3	40	101.6
2	51	5.1	20	50.8	41	104.1
2½	64	6.4	21	53.3	42	106.7
3	76	7.6	22	55.9	43	109.2
3½	89	8.9	23	58.4	44	111.8
4	102	10.2	24	61.0	45	114.3
4½	114	11.4	25	63.5	46	116.8
5	127	12.7	26	66.0	47	119.4
6	152	15.2	27	68.6	48	121.9
7	178	17.8	28	71.1	49	124.5
8	203	20.3	29	73.7	50	127.0

YARDS TO METERS

Yards	Meters	Yards	Meters	Yards	Meters	Yards	Meters	Yards	Meters
⅛	0.11	2⅛	1.94	4⅛	3.77	6⅛	5.60	8⅛	7.43
¼	0.23	2¼	2.06	4¼	3.89	6¼	5.72	8¼	7.54
⅜	0.34	2⅜	2.17	4⅜	4.00	6⅜	5.83	8⅜	7.66
½	0.46	2½	2.29	4½	4.11	6½	5.94	8½	7.77
⅝	0.57	2⅝	2.40	4⅝	4.23	6⅝	6.06	8⅝	7.89
¾	0.69	2¾	2.51	4¾	4.34	6¾	6.17	8¾	8.00
⅞	0.80	2⅞	2.63	4⅞	4.46	6⅞	6.29	8⅞	8.12
1	0.91	3	2.74	5	4.57	7	6.40	9	8.23
1⅛	1.03	3⅛	2.86	5⅛	4.69	7⅛	6.52	9⅛	8.34
1¼	1.14	3¼	2.97	5¼	4.80	7¼	6.63	9¼	8.46
1⅜	1.26	3⅜	3.09	5⅜	4.91	7⅜	6.74	9⅜	8.57
1½	1.37	3½	3.20	5½	5.03	7½	6.86	9½	8.69
1⅝	1.49	3⅝	3.31	5⅝	5.14	7⅝	6.97	9⅝	8.80
1¾	1.60	3¾	3.43	5¾	5.26	7¾	7.09	9¾	8.92
1⅞	1.71	3⅞	3.54	5⅞	5.37	7⅞	7.20	9⅞	9.03
2	1.83	4	3.66	6	5.49	8	7.32	10	9.14

INDEX